D0192720

Nick Skelton

Only Falls and Horses

GREENWATER
PUBLISHING

Copyright © Nick Skelton 2001

First published in Great Britain in 2001
by Greenwater Publishing
A division of Crystalsight Limited

All rights reserved. No part of this publication may be
reproduced, stored in a retrieval system, or transmitted, in any
form or by any means, electronic, mechanical, photocopying,
recording or otherwise, without the prior written permission
of the publishers.

The author asserts the moral right to be identified as the
author of this work

A CIP catalogue record for this book is available
from the British Library

ISBN 1-903267-05-6

Printed and bound in Great Britain by Mackays of Chatham PLC

Covers by: Richard Lappas

To Bettina,
  Thanks for always being there for me,
  and for putting up with me.

Contents

Introduction

I have worked as Nick Skelton's personal assistant for eleven years and when he told me he was writing his autobiography with the help of a well-known equestrian journalist, I was disappointed – I would have liked the opportunity to write it myself.

Several months later, the journalist decided that the task would prove too time-consuming and threw in the towel. Nick and I were in the office at Sanbrook Farm when he told me. We looked at each other and both had the same idea at the same time: 'Let's write it together.'

I have written equestrian articles, but the longest was 1,600 words and the publisher required 75,000 for this autobiography. We had only three-and-a-half months left to complete the book, during which time I would still have to fulfil my role as Nick's personal assistant – the prospect was daunting. Working for Nick wears me out at the best of times without the added hazard of having to write a book!

We put together a couple of chapters and sent them through to the publisher to see if they would accept the book being written by a virtually unknown author ... It turned out they liked the style.

Nick and I spent many hours closeted together in the office at Sanbrook Farm. Dredging up old memories was exhausting work and we stocked up with supplies before we started each session; we munched our way through dozens of packets of chocolate fingers, jam tarts, Crunch Creams and drank endless bottles of Coke.

I managed to get through the summer by adhering to Nick's own work ethic: there are seven working days in the week.

My thanks to the many people whose days were interrupted by

Nick calling them on their mobile phones to request help in remembering the finer points of detail which I pestered him for; to Janette for compiling the scrapbooks which proved invaluable; and special thanks to Nick's parents, David and Norma, without whom the early chapters would have been impossible to write.

And Nick – it has been a long-held ambition of mine to write a book; thanks to you, I have realised that ambition.

Mary Neal

Greenhill Farm
Warwickshire
August 2001

Acknowledgments

I would like to thank all the people who have contributed to my career over the twenty-seven years I competed: my parents, David and Norma, for buying me Oxo; Sarah Skelton, for supporting me when I decided to make a go of it on my own, and for giving me two terrific sons; Kenneth and Lesley Clawson; Ted and Liz Edgar; owners: Terry Clemence, Linda Jones, Gary Widdowson, Sally Mapleson, Tony Elliot, Sue and Freddie Welch, David Broome, Lord and Lady Harris, John, Pat and Lisa Hales, and even Joe Haller; my sponsors: Raffles Cigarettes, Burmah Castrol, Alan Paul Hairdressing, Virtual Village and Everest; all the staff who have cared for my horses over the years; and finally, my thanks to Mary Neal for helping me to write this book.

Foreword

BY DAVID NICHOLSON

I was highly honoured when Nick asked me to write the foreword to his autobiography, but thinking about it, it was probably because he has always been a frustrated National Hunt jockey.

He tells me that the first time we met was in 1970 when his father David had a horse in training with me, and even then Nick was doing his best to tell me how best to train it! Little did I realise that his original ambition at school was to come to me to be made into a jockey. However, that changed when he rode a few winners over coloured poles and got bitten by the show jumping bug. Fate obviously lent a helping hand in that job selection as he might have struggled to do the weight.

You will read about all the years of successful riding, the records are outstanding: Junior European Champion, World Cup Champion, three consecutive Hickstead Derby's, 137 appearances on the British Team are but a sprinkling.

Nick would probably agree that his career was moulded by Liz and Ted Edgar, with whom he spent twelve years before starting out on his own. Lots of people said that he wouldn't make the grade without the Edgars behind him – we all know the answer to those who doubted.

His horses were never taken for granted. Some of the best would have been Apollo, St James, Dollar Girl and Showtime, all of which had long, long careers at the top, while Tinka's Boy, who was brought out by Nick and sold abroad, has shown appreciation for his early care by becoming one of the best in the world. Hopes are High was coming to his peak when retirement was forced upon his jockey, so hopefully he will continue on the upgrade.

Nick's passion for racing got a real boost when he brought Certainly Strong – who carried his colours to plenty of success – while Oi Mother, who also won, was named with the owner's customary sense of humour, after my wife. He had noticed that whenever I needed to summon my wife, I would shout, 'Oi, Mother', which certainly kept her on her toes!

You might think that in such a cut-throat sport, there would be little time for others, not so with Nick. When Richard Dunwoody (a good mate) was at his wit's end at a turning point in his career, Nick organised a meeting for a few of us in the local pub to redirect him. He has always been very ready to help anyone in a fix and support or organise a fundraising event.

It is noticeable that those who get to the top have worked their way through every level of their particular trade. This is certainly true of Nick, whose horse-mastership is second to none, from the bottom upwards. I would hope that someone will have the sense to make good use of his knowledge in the future. Thankfully, with Daniel and Harry to step into his shoes, there should be no shortage of Skeltons in the ring in the future.

David Nicholson
August 2001

CHAPTER ONE
Making an Impact

Maybe had qualified for the Horse of the Year Show. In those days, horses had to win enough money to qualify to jump throughout the week and Maybe had done that as well as qualifying for the Grade C final and the Whitbread Young Riders. We had also qualified for the Butlins Championship that was on the Monday night. This was a great feat for a young horse, as Maybe was only about eight at the time.

The qualifiers for the Butlins Championship were held at the various Butlins Holiday Camps around the country: Skegness, Bognor Regis, Clacton, Filey, Pwhlleli, Minehead, all the good old British seaside resorts. We used to go to all of them, just for the day.

I was excited, I was now going to my first Horse of the Year Show as a rider; I was very keen to make an impact. And an impact I made!

Monday night used to be the first night of the Horse of the Year Show and there were some big classes, with invited foreign riders taking part. The Butlins Championship was being televised live by the BBC. It was my first time in the Wembley arena, and Maybe jumped clear in the first round. I thought that was great! A dream come true. But I was determined not to let it end there, with just one clear round.

In the jump-off, some fella called Alwin Schockemöhle came in riding a horse called Santa Monica, a big grey mare. I had never heard of him before but I soon realised he was Germany's best. He was winning, ahead on time. I didn't see him go but my trainer Ted Edgar told me to go for a slow clear as it was my first time, Maybe was a young horse and I would end up fourth or fifth.

As I went through the curtains I thought, 'Bollocks, who is this Alwin Schockemöhle anyway?' and set off down to the first at a fair clip, completely against Ted's orders, thinking, 'Well, if I win I'll be a hero.'

Maybe jumped the first few fences flying, we were clear and all we had left was the last line of a typical Alan Ball course: a triple bar off the corner, four strides to a double, vertical in, one stride, then an oxer out. This was one of only two final lines that Alan ever built in all the years he built at Wembley. That was what you had to train your horse to jump, and since then I have always trained my horses to jump triple bar, four strides, vertical, one stride, oxer. Now all I had to do was to jump that last line – we were flying, up on the clock. I turned back to the big triple bar on two strides and I missed; and I mean, missed.

We took off one too early, jumped straight into the middle of the triple bar and instead of pulling up before the double I kicked on for the four strides which were getting quite long by now. Again, we left the ground a bit early so we demolished the vertical and crashed the final oxer.

When I looked back down the line as I left, there wasn't a pole left standing. And most of the wings were down. It was like a Scud missile had shot down the centre of the Wembley Arena. It was my first appearance at Wembley and I had made an impact. But not the impact I had wanted to make.

The reception I received when I got back through the curtains was not too good. Ted Edgar dragged me off the horse shouting, 'You stupid little fucker, who do you think you are?' waving his finger at me constantly. The BBC outside camera at the back of the collecting ring was filming every minute of this tirade. Each night that week, at the start of the programme, the BBC showed Ted dragging me off Maybe, waving his finger at me. But, thankfully, without the commentary.

That was the first of many bollockings I had from Ted.

I took myself back to the stables and washed Maybe off and cleaned my tack and went to bed. Jill Tasker, with whom I had a few run-ins over the years, was especially pleased that I had had such a public telling off as she thought I was a cocky little kid.

For the next few days I kept a low profile; I wasn't seen out and about too much, I kept my head down and just did my usual job, gofering. Things improved as the week wore on. Maybe came out and won the Grade C Final and the following day won the Whitbread Young Riders Championship. We beat Cheryl Walker (now Grimes) riding Marlay Stetson, and third was Geoff Goodwin riding Latin Lady. Two more red rosettes!

I had got my confidence back and thought I had redeemed myself but although Ted was pleased, he never really forgave me for making such a mess that first night.

CHAPTER TWO

Early Years

I was due to be born on Christmas Day – hence my name, Nicholas. I guess my full name should have been Saint Nicklaus but I don't think that would have been very appropriate.

I'm told I jumped my first fence in December 1957. My parents had gone to a Boxing Day party at my Uncle Clifford's – the cars outside the house were parked awkwardly and my mum, who was heavily pregnant, was struggling to make her way to the front door. My dad said, 'Jump over the wall, it'll start the baby coming.' She obligingly did so but it didn't do any good, I wasn't born for another four days.

My parents were living at The Cedars in Exhall, Coventry and it was 5.30 a.m. on 30 December when my mum went into labour. She had opted to have me at home so after a few hours my dad telephoned the midwife and asked her to call round.

She came in, looked at my mum and said, 'You'll be all right, I'll go home and do my washing and I'll be back.' So off she went and came back a few hours later. She examined my mum and said, 'I'm going home to do the ironing,' and disappeared for another hour or two.

The next time she came back she announced, 'I think I'll go back and get the tea ready,' but my dad's nerves were now stretched to breaking point and he shouted, 'You're not going anywhere and that's that.' Then he stood across the doorway with his arms outstretched to stop her from leaving.

He was absolutely right, as I was born at teatime, just when the midwife would have been at home making the tea. My mum says I was a big baby, 9lb, with fair hair and I already looked a month old when I was born. Incidentally, that 9lb was my lowest-ever riding weight! By all accounts I was a good baby and slept pretty well every night, a talent I still have in my forties.

I got my first pony when I was only 18 months old. Dad didn't want me to have a pony so young but Mum was determined and got her own way – I was presented with Oxo who was only two years old at the time and, being the same age, we grew up together. Oxo cost £40 and was bought from Sue Bond. In those early days he was kept at my Uncle John's although we did have a paddock at the back of the house.

Because my dad owned a pharmacy, everyone has always assumed that I was a one-off as regards liking horses, but both my parents rode and my mum is from a very horsey family. My great-grandfather had dray horses and at Easter they used to do special day trips in the four-in-hand carriage from Coventry to Stratford. They were coal merchants but had high steppers as well as the dray horses. They even had a horse-drawn hearse, which was, of course, used for funerals.

My mum, Norma, hunted with the Atherstone although she admits, 'I was off the pony more than I was on!' She had a grey Arab pony called Bob when she was a child and rode out with her uncles, Charlie and Walter. My dad rode when he was young as well and his great-grandparents had their own pack of foxhounds up in Yorkshire.

My parents have known each other since they were 15 years old and were the best of friends. I'll let Mum tell you: 'I met David Skelton at the Church Fellowship and lived next door to his grandfather, so we saw a tremendous amount of each other. When David was eighteen he had to go and do his National Service and was due to leave for Brecon for ten weeks' training when we had decided we wanted to get engaged. Our parents weren't keen but David sold his clothes to raise the money to buy me a ring. We went to Leicester to buy the ring and Nick's sister Sally has it now.'

After completing the first ten weeks of army training, Dad was posted to Egypt. He chose to go there because his own father had been in Egypt during the First World War as an officer in the Royal Flying Corps. Grandad had flown Tiger Moths from Cairo down to

Suez and was one of only a handful of survivors from Warwickshire in those days.

It was 1950 and Dad sailed from Liverpool on the Empire Test, which took over three weeks to get to Port Said. Upon arrival he was posted to Ismailia where he was based with five others and a couple of veterinary officers. He travelled with the veterinary officers all over Egypt, from Cairo to Port Said, and from Port Said down to Suez, hunting down rabid dogs. When they found a dog that was foaming at the mouth – a classic sign of rabies – the veterinary officer would shoot the dog and then remove the brain to analyse it, to see whether or not the dog definitely had rabies. Some dogs foam at the mouth even when they haven't got rabies, but – according to my dad – the breath of a rabid dog is putrid.

On one occasion they were called out to examine a dog that belonged to an army officer's family. The dog was shot and the brain removed which showed that it did have rabies. Tragically, the dog had already passed on the rabies to the wife and three children and they all died dreadful deaths. The officer was, of course, absolutely devastated. It just shows how important their work was.

When Dad wasn't working with the veterinary officers, he used to go out exercising the army mules, riding one and leading two. He and his five colleagues would take eighteen mules out into the desert. They were very careful to check the weather forecasts for sandstorms but if they got caught in one they would stop, survey their surroundings and then stand facing in the direction of home. This way, when the storm was over they would know which way to go because after a sandstorm the scenery changes completely, sand dunes move and the whole horizon is different.

The army base was the base camp for all the mules and horses that the army bought in the Middle East, most of which came in from Cyprus or Nicosia. The army never paid more than £30 for a mule or a horse and they would be brought back to Port Said by boat. Although the army had transport they didn't have enough for all the horses and mules so the ones left over would be ridden back to the base camp, about 90 miles, right down along the Suez Canal.

The base also served as a Riding Club for the different services: soldiers, airmen, the navy; they all used to go out there and ride. A few years before my dad was out in Egypt, the late Harry Llewellyn had served there and used to ride a horse called Saracen. Saracen won show jumping competitions all over Egypt and Harry Llewellyn wanted to take the horse back to England with him, but couldn't afford to. By all accounts, Harry always said that Saracen was equally good, if not better, than his great horse Foxhunter.

After eighteen months, Dad got himself back to England. For one thing, he was to be demobbed, and for another, it was the start of the Korean War. There was only one boat leaving for England from Port Said and he managed to book his own passage, otherwise he would have ended up going on to Korea where they needed the mules that had been arriving at the base camp for some time, ready for the war. He got back to England with only a few days left to serve but the government added on another six months' service because of the Korean War. So he had to do two years' National Service instead of the usual eighteen months, finishing up with another six months at Melton Mowbray.

When, finally, he finished his National Service in 1952, Dad went to work in his parents' pharmacy in Bedworth. The shop had opened in 1852 and had been in the family ever since, so when he went to work there it was exactly one hundred years after it had first opened. He took it over in 1978 when my grandparents retired. Dad wasn't a qualified pharmacist, he employed the pharmacists and ran the shop.

My parents were married for four years before they had me and in the early years they lived in a flat over an ironmonger's shop in Longford, Coventry. They bought a brand-new Ford van, which cost £209 but only came with a driver's seat. They had to buy an extra seat for the passenger! I can't imagine having to buy seats as an optional extra these days.

I have always had a talent for getting into scrapes, and my dad tells this story: 'One day I was cleaning the downstairs windows at The Cedars. Nick was only two and he was outside helping me. I can't remember why but I walked off for just a few minutes and while I was gone Nick climbed on the stool to have a go at cleaning the nearest window. He couldn't manage, of course, and fell off the stool. He had a huge bump on his forehead and was all black down one side of his face! A couple of days later we went on holiday to Blackpool and while there someone asked him how he got the bump on his head. He told them, 'My dad, he hit me!' which was a complete lie and earned me a terrible scowl.'

When I was very young I had a hobbyhorse called Mobo. The legs were on springs and it was a fearsome beast. I used to ride it like kids ride mountain bikes nowadays. I could make it rear and buck, I would have it leaping all over the place and I used to fall off it all the time. I'm convinced that riding Mobo taught me to stay on and to keep in balance with my horses. Until something went wrong in the year 2000 ...

When I graduated from Mobo, Mum taught me to ride Oxo who was now kept in the paddock at the back of the house. I had a couple of grooms from the beginning – my parents! My riding clothes were always laid out ready to put on and the pony was always ready for me to ride. I didn't have to get up early and go outside to do my pony before school – Mum always did it for me, although at weekends I used to clean the bits of Oxo that I could reach. I would pick out his feet and brush his fetlocks.

Harry and Daniel, my sons, were just the same when they were very small. They would follow one of my groom's into the stable when they brought in one of my good show jumpers after exercise and start taking off it's boots and bandages and run their hands knowledgeably along its lower legs, asking questions all the time.

I was sent to Coventry Preparatory School where I didn't do well academically but I won everything in sport. I was always the first back from cross-country runs, but sometimes I was spotted getting on the bus! In those days I thought that winning was all that mattered, not how you did it and that philosophy has stuck with me until this very day.

At one sports day I won five cups and so far as I am aware I still hold the one hundred yard sprint record at Coventry Prep. The headmaster, Mr Phipps, once had my dad in to complain, 'Nicholas doesn't train hard enough, he doesn't put everything into it.' But my dad said to him, 'When it comes to sports day he puts every possible effort into winning, and that's what matters.' It was true. I never could see the point of putting in a lot of effort beforehand, just do it on the day. Win when there is something to win, that's what I thought.

In the school holidays I would ride about a mile down the road to the pharmacy where Dad worked. In those days there were no houses along the road and very few cars. I rode up the entry, round the back and put Oxo in the garage – where Dad kept some straw and water – until it was time to ride back home again.

Oxo and I started going to the local gymkhanas, mainly Exhall and Bedworth, Ansty, and Shilton. At first I was on the leading rein and my dad always found the fastest runners for me – Dave Docker and Roger Abbott were two of the best. I also used to ride Taffy who belonged to Roger. Taffy was difficult to load and Tess, Roger's mum, used to give it one up the backside with a long tom to get it in the horsebox.

I met Stuart Crutchlow at Exhall and Bedworth gymkhana. He was a few years older than me and we became the best of friends. He lived a mile down the road from me in Bedworth where his parents owned the bakery. His Dad, who I called Uncle Fred, used to run a delivery service in his bread van. Stuart would go with him and I would be looking out of the window waiting for them. When the van came past I would jump in and off we'd go.

His mother, Aunty Millie, used to run the baker's shop and every Saturday morning we would end up back at the shop and any leftover bread rolls were made into ham rolls. Stuart's mother made the best ham rolls in Bedworth. Stuart and I were inseparable, looking forward to Sundays when we would go to the local gymkhanas together and play havoc.

One day especially springs to mind – it was at Exhall and Bedworth gymkhana. We had a few hours to spare between gymkhana events so we decided to go off, as kids do, playing up the trees. There was a stream close by and we wanted to see if we could cross it by climbing across the branches of an overhanging tree. So we scrambled up the tree and climbed across the branch when all of a sudden the bough broke! In we both went, up to our necks in cold water! Jodhpurs, jodhpur boots, everything was soaked. We didn't get a very good reception from our parents when we got back, covered in slime.

Oxo and I won hundreds of rosettes together, sometimes as many as five red rosettes in a weekend, which was pretty good. I couldn't wait for the next Sunday to come around so I could win some more. It was red rosettes I always wanted, for first place; not blue or green, which are second and third. I got to like the idea of winning, something that has stuck with me to this day.

Oxo was fiercely competitive, but he wasn't perfect. I did the Fancy Dress class once, dressed as Ivanhoe – Oxo hated brass bands and as we went into the ring the band started up. Oxo reared up and I fell off. My outfit was held together with pins and the fancy dress fell apart. With pins sticking in all over me, I screamed the place down and my mother thought I was injured, but it was just the pins.

When I was six we moved from The Cedars to Holly Lodge in Berkswell where we had 24 acres of land and two-and-a-half acres of garden. I thought it was heaven – all this land to ride on, hedges and rails to jump. Oxo and I were now in paradise. Oxo had the paddock at the bottom of the garden and there were stables at the top near the house.

My mother became pregnant shortly after we moved to Holly Lodge and as my parents weren't keen to repeat the stressful experience of me being born at home, my sister Sally was born in hospital on 12 June 1965.

When Sally was five years old she decided she wanted to learn how to ride. We were in the garden playing together and I put her up on Oxo. I was leading Sally around the garden on Oxo and then decided to let go. There was a privet hedge in the garden; it was only about three feet high. Well, every time Oxo had seen the privet hedge, we always jumped it, so as I let go, Oxo spotted the privet hedge. He trotted off and over he went … Sally hit the floor in a big heap and disappeared into the house crying. That just about ended Sally's riding career.

CHAPTER THREE

I Wanna be a Jockey

Every year, my mother's father, Grandad Brindley, used to take me to Gold Cup day at Cheltenham. We would go with my dad who has always been keen on racing. I used to get the day off school and my dad would put me up on his shoulders so I could see over the crowds. I have been to every Gold Cup since, but nowadays I usually watch it from the bar, as my friend Aiden Murphy is a bad influence on me!

I saw Arkle win all of his three Gold Cups. At the age of seven I thought that horse was the most fantastic horse I had ever seen. I remember I was absolutely devastated when Arkle got injured and broke his pastern. I sent him a get-well card and a box of sugar lumps. I couldn't believe it when I received a letter and a photograph from his owner– Anne, Duchess of Westminster – thanking me for the sugar lumps. I see her now at the races and remind her I was the little boy that she was good enough to write back to. She is one of the nicest ladies you would ever wish to meet and is still getting winners today.

Watching the steeplechasing inspired me to want to be a jockey. The excitement of jumping at speed really thrilled me at that time. The first thing I would do when I got home from Cheltenham was tack up Oxo. I would shorten my stirrups so my knees were up and race all over the 24 acres – jumping hedges and rails trying to see if I could get him to fall! But he never fell, he was too clever. Every time I went over the privet hedge into the garden (where Sally fell off), my mother would yell out of the kitchen window, 'You're going to hurt yourself!' but I ignored her and raced on.

When I was seven years old, my parents took me to the Horse of the Year Show at Wembley. It was the year they had a parade of the Grand National winners. I vividly remember my dad taking me to the stables and asking the stable lad if I could sit on Nicholas Silver who had won in 1961. The lad took me into the stable and threw me up on Nicholas Silver. It made my day.

I never used to go inside at Wembley to watch the classes; I would be outside watching David Broome and Harvey Smith riding on the black ash warm-up arena. They were my childhood show jumping heroes but it never occurred to me that I would be going there jumping one day myself – I wanted to be a steeplechase jockey. Pat Taffe and Terry Biddlecombe, they were my jockey heroes.

Although we had moved away, Stuart and I still used to meet up at the gymkhanas at the weekends and during holidays we would stay over at each other's houses, taking our ponies with us.

Living in a new area we started going to different shows: Crackley, Tile Hill, and Keresley. I remember one time at the Kenilworth Show we had won pretty much everything in our class (Oxo was only 11.2 hands), so towards the end of the afternoon we went in the Open classes that had better prize money. Oxo was lining up alongside rangy thoroughbred-type 14.2s ridden by much older boys and I was trying to elbow my way into pole position when somebody in the crowd shouted, 'Give the little 'un a chance!' to which someone else answered, 'Nah, hold that little bugger back! I've seen him at Exhall and Bedworth!'

Although I kept Oxo all his life until he died when he was 39 years old, I had more ponies when I outgrew him. The first pony I had after Oxo was very naughty and used to run off with me. One time he dashed off up the muckheap and ended up in the wire. He frightened me to death. The pony was a liability so it was sent back and my parents bought me a stunning black pony from Major Long called Prince Tarquin.

Tarquin was my first proper jumping pony. He was 13.2 and I was 11 years old. I used 45-gallon oil drums for jump wings, or anything else that would support a pole. Rails were just bits of wood, telegraph poles, anything. In those days if I'd had a 12ft pole, I would have cut it in half and made two fences.

Tarquin could jump quite well so we started going to Affiliated shows and joined the British Show Jumping Association (BSJA). He was also good at cross-country so we went to Hunter Trials as well. I remember one day doing the cross-country at Meriden Show. Somehow, Tarquin fell at a fence and when he got up he trod on my collarbone and broke it. I have been very lucky and wasn't injured in a riding accident again until 1999 when I shattered my collarbone in a fall at Solihull.

Stuart had now got a good 14.2 pony called Seamus and we were travelling together, going to a lot of Affiliated shows further afield. Uncle Fred used to drive us in an old Thames Trader horsebox. Tarquin was going well and winning a lot of 13.2 classes.

I remember my first trip to Hickstead in 1968, when I was only 11 years old. Stuart had qualified for the Junior Foxhunter Finals with Seamus and there were also 13.2 classes down there so I took Tarquin. Setting off to Hickstead was a major adventure in those days; there were very few motorways – no M40 or M25, just the M1– and it took about six-and-a-half hours to get there. We arrived at Hickstead in the dark and had to unload, muck out the lorry and bed the ponies down by torchlight. We had an old gas ring for a cooker and a canister of water for washing and drinking. Uncle Fred was asleep on the luton over the cab and Stuart and I had sleeping bags in the back on the straw.

Stuart finished second in the Foxhunter Finals that year and I had some good places in the 13.2 classes, but I wasn't winning at that level, which annoyed me. A couple of years later I jumped Tarquin in the Main Ring at Hickstead in the 13.2 Championship. We didn't win but a lad called Johnny Haynes came first with Ballyshan; I think he won the 13.2 Championship of Great Britain three years in succession. Johnny went on to become a good National Hunt jockey but, unfortunately, he had a bad fall racing which finished his career. He was paralysed and is still in a wheelchair to this day. I often see him at the Horse of the Year Show at Wembley.

When I outgrew Tarquin he was sold to James Aird in Scotland who bought him for one of his children who had come out of 12.2s. They never sold him because they kept him in the family as a succession of brothers and sisters rode him. Tarquin was a champion in Scotland and as far as I know he stayed with the Airds until he died.

After Coventry Prep School I went to Bablake Boys School, also in Coventry. It was a good school academically and I had to pass an entrance exam to get in. God knows how I did that.

I was well behaved at school but played truant a lot. My dad took me to school every morning and then I would go and find a telephone and call Mum and ask her to come and pick me up because I wasn't well. She fell for it every time and always used to turn up.

In the summer of 1971 my parents separated. I was thirteen years old. Holly Lodge – the paradise I shared with Oxo – was sold and my dad bought Odnaull End Farm in Berkswell, which had six acres of land and stables, so my ponies and I went to live with Dad. Sally, my little sister, was only seven years old so she went to live with my mum. Sally and I are very close despite being separated when we were young.

My parents divorced in 1972 and Mum subsequently married Derek Jones (who is really great with my kids) and they had a son together. My brother Michael Jones is now with Alison Bradley who used to ride Endeavour and was on the silver medal European Championship Team in St Gallen in 1995 when I was riding Dollar Girl.

My dad and I were living on our own at Odnaull End Farm and he no longer drove me to school. I was supposed to go on the train from Berkswell Station. We lived by the old disused railway line and I would walk down the track to the station. Sometimes I would hide behind the hedge and watch until Dad went to work and then go back into the yard and ride my ponies. Dad never came home from work until after I would have been home from school so he didn't know I played truant until I wrote this book!

In 1972, my dad's partner, Janette Southall, moved into Odnaull End Farm with us. She had a thoroughbred mare that bred a foal; Janette quite fancied the idea of the two-year-old going flat racing so a friend of Dad's, Lol Weaver, suggested that we take it to David Nicholson at Condicote. The two-year-old went into training and ran on the flat at Doncaster and was useless.

As a result Dad asked David to look out for another horse for him to buy. David found Christmas Comet who went on to win a couple of races over hurdles for him. In the meantime, while going over to David Nicholson's this idea of being a jockey started to take a hold as I had the occasional ride out, and I thought, 'This has gotta be the life for me!' – How wrong I was!

We had a handyman and he would cut holes in the hedge and build fences for me to jump the ponies over. I had post and rails, ditches toward, ditches behind, the lot. He was so helpful.

At Odnaull End Farm we had a couple of chicken houses where I kept chickens and also some lambs. I had two orphan lambs, which I hand-reared and bottle-fed. They were so friendly, they were like pets, but when they got to killing size I asked my Dad if someone else could take them to market, I couldn't handle it.

My friend Greg Parsons lived just up the lane in Balsall Common and we were always coming up with some new moneymaking scheme to supplement our pocket money. We decided to use the two biggest chicken sheds for rearing capons and bought a load from market to get them fat for Christmas. We looked after them so well that a couple of them put on so much weight that they went off their legs. Finally, come Christmas it was time to kill and dress them. We were good at killing them and did it quickly and painlessly but plucking and dressing was another matter. Those capons were plucked in a fashion, and to whoever ended up having feathers in their dinner on Christmas Day, I apologise profusely!

In the winter I used to go to indoor shows at Balsall Common Equestrian Centre, which was owned by the Harper family. Gwen Harper is the mother of Katie Meacham the three-day event rider who was killed so tragically a couple of years ago. Gwen's sister, Jean Harper, is married to John Sillett who was Manager of Coventry City when they won the FA Cup final in 1986.

It was at Balsall Common that I met the Clawsons. Ken Clawson is now the show jumping trainer for the British Three-Day Event Team. One day, my dad was talking to Ken's girlfriend, Lesley, about ponies. They owned a few 13.2 ponies and Lesley asked if I would ride some of them. They had three 13.2s; a roan pony called

Kimberley Rook, a grey pony called Bullet and a coloured pony called Hanky Panky. I duly accepted the ride on these ponies but with Dad being so busy at work and me at home on my own, Lesley and Kenneth (as he was always called) took me in hand.

They lived at Leire over in Leicestershire so I had to make my own way there. Stuart, who was now seventeen, had a driving licence and he used to be my chauffeur, driving me over in the evenings to ride the ponies. We travelled constantly to shows with the Clawsons and I would take Prince Tarquin along with me so I was riding four 13.2s.

I first met Lizzie Harris at Balsall Common as well. She was my kind of girl and we became great friends, although it was never any more than that. Honest! She had a good 14.2-jumping pony called Just William. Dad and Janette became friendly with Lizzie's parents and we used to spend a lot of time at each other's houses. She is now married with two children and lives in California. I went on a riding trip in New Zealand and on the way back I called in to see her at her home on Malibu Beach.

I also met Johnny Wrathall at Balsall Common. Stuart, Johnny and I became like the three musketeers. Johnny was also quite a bit older than me so between the two of them they thoroughly led me astray! Now I understand why my headmaster used to write on my school report: 'Nick is easily led.' I was.

Johnny used to live at South Kilworth in Northamptonshire, so he was travelling some distance to come to Balsall Common. His dad was a good producer of young horses, his most famous being Pennwood Forgemill who later went on to win the European Championships with Paddy McMahon.

Mr Wrathall was a farmer and Stuart and I used to drive over to Johnny's on a Friday night. They always had a yard full of ponies and horses and Saturday morning we used to help milk the cows and then we would go hunting with the Pytchley. Johnny's Dad used to wake us up at six o'clock in the morning with the strongest tea I have ever tasted. It was like drinking tar; so strong it was black.

South Kilworth was not far from Leire so on a Saturday night the three of us would go over to the Clawsons and go out. I was only 13, going out at night with two seventeen-year-olds! I blame Stuart and Johnny for the fact that later on in life I got into so much trouble with the girls!

Prince Tarquin was sold when I moved out of 13.2s at the age of fourteen. Uncle Fred told Dad that he knew where there was a nice pony but the girl who rode it, Louise Spencer, wasn't getting on that well with it. We saw it at Balsall Common and I had a ride on the pony Calibas, and jumped a trial class; it jumped two clear rounds. Dad asked Uncle Fred if he thought we could buy it.

Louise's father lived close to Uncle Fred so they knew each other and Uncle Fred asked him if he would sell it. Mr Spencer replied, 'I'll sell the pony, Fred, as long as I get my money back,' but didn't give him a price. Uncle Fred told my dad to make out a cheque for £400 and he dropped it off at Spencer's. The cheque was for the right amount and Mr Spencer asked Uncle Fred how he knew how much he had paid for the pony. Uncle Fred told him, 'I know everything sold in this area and for how much!'

Towards the end of my time at Bablake School, especially the last eighteen months, I kept taking time off because I was going to shows with the Clawsons, Stuart and Johnny. I missed a lot of schooling when I was fourteen. The teachers complained that I always had my mind on ponies; they were all I was interested in. The headmaster even called my parents in and told them but it made no difference to me. School came second fiddle to the ponies. I couldn't wait to be fifteen and leave school.

The Clawsons now had several 14.2 ponies, including a good piebald pony called On The Move. The usual rider, Nigel Wood, had broken his leg so I got the ride and took it to Hickstead. It was a good pony, On The Move.

Hickstead was the place to go. They held four meetings every year and we were travelling to all of them. Stuart and Johnny were both on horses now. They were good riders and Johnny went on to become an amateur jockey. Sometimes, if I went badly in a class, Ken Clawson would lock me in the caravan and I would climb out of the window to escape. The three of us used to go up the Castle pub and every night I would get thrown out by the landlord Terry Sherman because I was under age. He used to throw me out of the front door and I would go round and come in the back door and bury myself in the thick of the crowd so he couldn't see me.

Afterwards, we would go back to the horseboxes at the show ground and have parties. I remember one time in a two-horse trailer seeing this sleeping bag moving; I pulled the cover back and there was this lad with a smile on his face; I asked, 'Who are you?' and he replied, 'John.' I went on, 'John who?' and he said, 'John Whitaker.' And that was the first time we met. I mustn't tell you whom he was with, but she was a pretty girl, and judging her on conformation, from what I could see she was a good sort!

CHAPTER FOUR
Edgar Years

Calibas and I were not seeing eye too eye. He had started to get a mind of his own. Nothing specific – just having a fence down, running out, rushing his fences, I couldn't hold him, the odd refusal; other than that, everything else was fine.

Lol Weaver – who incidentally, has been Chief Steward at the Horse of the Year Show and Olympia for as long as I can remember – suggested that Dad took Calibas and me over to some friends of his, Ted and Liz Edgar. Liz, who is David Broome's sister, and Ted were both professional show jumpers, and Lol thought they could put me right with my pony.

Off we went to Leek Wootton for a lesson. On arrival, Ted was not there, he was away and Liz tried to help me with the pony. She put me right on what I was doing wrong but it didn't make a lot of difference to Calibas' ability. He simply wasn't up to the job; I think we had got to the end of the road.

When Ted arrived home he asked Liz how 'that kid' had got on with his pony. She told him, 'The pony was useless, but I think the kid's got potential.'

A week or so later the phone rang at home; it was Ted Edgar asking if I would like to go and help them at the shows at weekends if I wasn't away jumping myself. My ambition was still to be a jockey so I wasn't all that bothered but I thought I would give it a try. I wasn't allowed to ride anything, this wasn't like the Clawsons. I was cleaning tack, polishing Ted's boots, holding horses, just helping generally. Ted and Liz's daughter, Marie, was two years old and I used to lead her around on her little bay pony, Jewel. Later on when Marie was about four years old, I loaned Oxo to her and she competed him in lead rein classes and she benefited from the same good grounding as I had had. I would never ever have sold Oxo, but I loaned him to several good child riders. Anne Backhouse's children had him and also Althea Barclay's children used to hunt him. The last person to have him on loan was Jeff McVean's daughter Emily. Both my children learned to ride on him. He was a good old soldier.

The first show I went to with the Edgars was a two-day show at Nottingham Racecourse. I was sleeping in the front of the horsebox; Ted and Liz had a caravan. Their groom, Fenella Power, aka Hob, was sleeping in the horsebox as well. Suddenly, in the middle of the night, the door burst open and an older lad walked in. He picked me up in my sleeping bag and slung me out on to the grass! Then he slammed the door shut and locked it and I couldn't get back in until feeding time at seven o'clock the next morning. Just as well it was a summer show as I had taken my sleeping bag and slept under the horsebox on the grass.

In the morning I thought, 'I must find out who that was'; after further investigation I came up with the culprit's name: Tim Grubb. Grubby later went on to represent Great Britain at several Olympic Games riding Night Murmur at the 1980 substitute Games in Rotterdam, Linky in 1984 at Los Angeles and Denizen in 1992 at Barcelona. He then took US citizenship and now rides for the USA.

That same summer I remember going to the Bath and West Show at Shepton Mallet. Again, I was just helping. I was everybody's gofer, even the grooms treated me as their gofer. One lunchtime in the caravan, Ted was having his lunch and he said, 'Pass me the salad cream.' I said, 'We haven't got any salad cream.' So he told me, 'Well go and get some off that Banky next door'. Banky was Trevor Banks.

Well, I had heard and seen this Trevor Banks before. I thought he was a big, ignorant, arrogant man. Harvey Smith and Mick Saywell rode for him at that time. I thought, 'I don't wanna go in his caravan. I daren't go in there and ask for salad cream.' They intimidated me. I knocked on the door and there was a big growl, 'Come in.' So I crept in and Banky snarled, 'Whadda you want?'

By this time I was getting a name around the shows for being the kid that Ted had got as a gofer, so Banky knew I was with them next door. I said, 'Have you got any salad cream?' and he replied, 'Yeah, and it's got "please" written on the fucking label!' I thought, 'Oh shit,' I had been so frightened I'd forgotten to say please!

I helped at Edgars' yard at weekends for the next six months but now I had the odd ride, walking about the collecting ring. Ted sent me a horse to ride at home, The Red Baron, an Australian horse brought over by John Fahey. He asked if I would like to keep him at home and ride him in a few Young Riders Classes, which I did. He was a nice horse, not too careful but he wasn't difficult to ride.

Then Ted sent me a dun horse called Timmie on which Liz had competed quite successfully, this was a good horse for me at that time. Dad took me around the shows and I was still jumping my pony and the horses at local shows, and then at weekends when I wasn't competing I travelled to shows with the Edgars. I went to the Horse of the Year Show at Wembley just helping, leading horses up, cleaning tack, that sort of thing.

That winter Ted and Liz were going to a show in Switzerland at Davos, jumping on snow. I had just celebrated my fifteenth birthday and it was the first time I had been abroad and I had to get a passport. We set off to Davos taking Everest Make Do and Boomerang for Liz, and Ted took Everest Peak and Snaffles. We travelled in the horsebox with David Broome who was one of my childhood heroes. I remember being most impressed that I would be travelling with him! David was riding Manhattan and Ballywillwill. Pam and Lionel Dunning made up the team.

When we arrived in Davos, I had never been in such cold weather in all my life. The horses were stabled in an indoor school in standing stalls made of poles slung together with rope. It was so cold you wouldn't believe it. The outside air froze the hairs in your nose, it was dreadful. I was gasping for breath. I was glad I'd had a shower before leaving home because it was the last one I had before I got back. It was too cold to wash. All I did was put more clothes on each day.

The horsebox froze solid and Ted had to get a mechanic out with a pair of heating bellows to thaw the engine. After we got it started we left it running for four days and four nights until it was time to come home. The grooms and I were sleeping in the lorry and I was thinking to myself, 'I hope I don't get a repeat of the Nottingham Show because it's too cold to sleep under the lorry!' But I was OK, I was sharing the lorry with a lad who wasn't that way inclined.

With the jumping being on snow, the horses had to have four studs in each hoof and the back stud was a two-inch long spike. Guess what my job was? Yep, you got it. I was up at five o'clock every morning studding six horses up, so that's four studs, four feet, six horses, a total of 96 studs. Classes started at eight o'clock in the morning, before the sun came up and melted the snow, and the last class was over by three in the afternoon. And then it was back to the studs, taking them all out again. I now consider that to have been my apprenticeship in studding!

My studding must have been up to scratch because Ted and Liz asked if I would like to go and work for them when I left school. I thought, 'Anything rather than school,' and thought it would do until I could get myself over to David Nicholson's and start being a jockey.

I mentioned this job offer to my headmaster and his words were: 'As you have missed so much school with shows, I think it is better that you pursue your outdoor activities rather than continue your academic career, if that's what you want.' I thought, 'That's good enough for me,' and left school at the end of the Easter term in 1972 without bothering to take my O' levels. I was fifteen years old.

I did not realise that this was to be the start of thirteen years' hard labour.

My first wage packet was £7 per week. My dad used to drive me to Edgars every day, seven days a week; it was years before I knew there are only five working days in a week, I always thought there were seven! And, by the way, I still think there are seven.

I would arrive at seven o'clock; it was like being in the army, everything happened by the clock. Seven o'clock feeding and mucking out the straw beds, every horse had one clean bale of straw every morning. There were eighteen stables and they had to be finished by eight o'clock. Feeding, mucking out, bedding down, buckets washed, all done by eight. We had three horses each. The muckheap was carted and 'coned', stacked properly, not just thrown up. The banks were two or three feet high around the wall, water buckets were filled, hay nets were filled, good old-fashioned stuff.

In December of that first winter at Edgars I turned sixteen. I was now old enough to legally ride a moped and that would save my dad driving me back and forth every day, so we went over to Halfords and bought one. It was yellow and I was very proud of it. The first thing I did was ride over to Coventry where my mother was living to show her. She inspected the moped and then I said I had to be going. She told me to be careful and watch what I was doing, as mothers do, and as I drove away, I turned around to wave goodbye to her and ran smack straight into a tree, tipped it upside down, and I fell off.

I used to ride that moped over to Edgars in rain, hail, and snow, no matter what the weather, I always managed to get to work. If I was five minutes late arriving, Ted would greet me, 'Good afternoon, having a half day are we?' and walk off. The problem is that if it was raining, it took me five minutes to get all my waterproof gear on in the morning so I was often five minutes late.

I was so pleased when I was seventeen and got a car licence. I got my first car, a Ford Escort, and didn't have to get wet any more.

There was no question of my horses not being done in time for breakfast. If I was a minute or two late I got a bollocking off Ted but Liz always made sure I still got my breakfast. The only reason I stayed there so long was that Liz was so good to me. Ted used to make me cook his breakfast, clean his boots, fetch his Woodbines – 'Oi, kid, fags. Go and fetch my fags.' And off I would go to fetch his Woodbines. If ever the drains were blocked in the stables, Ted would shout, 'Where's that kid?' and I would roll up my sleeves and put my arm down the drain.

Ted always referred to me as 'that kid,' just like he did the first day I took Calibas there for a lesson. He gave me the dirtiest, messiest jobs on the yard, jobs that the grooms wouldn't have done. But Liz used to keep the peace between us and she kept the whole thing going. She deserves a medal for perseverance and it should be as big as a dustbin lid.

Breakfast was at eight o'clock in the house; a bowl of cornflakes and a piece of toast with marmalade. And I must admit, the tea was much better than Mr Wrathall used to make! Ted used to go and get the milk from the next-door neighbours farm in his black mini pick-up. We had fresh, unpasteurised milk every day, straight from the cow. The farmer was Gordon Williams, whose son John Williams is now my vet. If I went with Ted I used to try and get into the dairy first so I could fill the milk can with the cream from the top of the vat because that always tasted better on my cornflakes.

At 8.45 a.m. it was everybody out back on the yard, tacking up and riding. I was still riding Timmie but The Red Baron had disappeared somewhere.

In those days they had a small indoor school with a flat roof approximately 12ft high, 80ft long, and maybe 40ft wide – very small. The surface was dirt and shavings. Mostly we worked the horses outside on the grass. It was a good field, a very sandy surface that drained well. We only rode indoors when it rained. If there were three or four of us riding all at the same time the horses used to go round like they were on the wall of death at the fair!

Monday was a rest day for the horses and they went out in the paddocks. Tuesday would be hacking, taking it easy. Ted had a big farm, 350 acres, so we rode mostly on the farm, with very little roadwork.

Wednesday was a workday for the horses, flat work and fitness work and then Thursday they had a jump. Friday we were off to a show for the weekend. It is a system that I still use. The great thing about being there was that the discipline and tidiness instilled in me by Ted has stood me in good stead throughout my life.

Monday was a really bad day for me. Rugby market used to be on a Monday and my first job on Monday morning was to tack up two horses and Ted and I would ride around the farm and round up all the sheep. We would put them in a pen and Ted's farm manager Fred Wilson – who is still there – would pull out the lambs that were ready for market. Then the lambs would be loaded into the lorry and Fred took them off to market.

I quite enjoyed going to market; it was like having a few hours off. As soon as we arrived we would have a cup of coffee because on Mondays we had missed out on breakfast. By eleven we were back at the yard and every Monday morning, every Monday morning, my job was to wash the horseboxes. They had to be immaculate; they were washed inside, outside, polished and vacuumed.

I also had to wash Ted's car, a red Mercedes coupé. Washing the car was okay, but I hated vacuuming those hairy car seats where their three Corgi dogs had been sitting. The dogs would sit on the rear parcel shelf and rub their noses on the back window, so every week I had to clean the glass. Why Ted didn't just have one of those toy dogs that nod their heads in the back window, I don't know. At least that wouldn't have made such a mess.

And then I had to vacuum up the pile of cigarette ash that had built up over the week because Ted refused to use the ashtray. He used to flick it on the carpet on the driver's side. It was a bad day, Monday.

Mind you, I got to like those Corgis because they were great telltales. Whenever Ted was coming down the yard those dogs would start barking so I knew it was time to get to my feet and start looking busy!

CHAPTER FIVE

Hunting

I was riding a new horse, which was to prove to be the first of my great horses and put me on the road to stardom. The horse was called Maybe.

Ted saw Maybe at Southport Flower Show in the collecting ring where Harvey Smith and Paul Darragh were trying it. Harvey allegedly said, 'It'll never be a jumper as long as it's got a hole up its arse,' and didn't buy it. Later on in 1977 I went on to beat Harvey in a jump-off for Leading Show Jumper of the Year with Maybe – I bet he wished it hadn't got that hole up his arse any more!

Ted went to try the horse at Mark Chambers' place in Cheshire and bought it from Freddie and Gill Cottam. Maybe was Irish by a stallion called Love and Marriage out of an Irish Draft mare.

Maybe wasn't the easiest of horses, he had a nappy streak in him. Ted maintained, 'I paid £500 for his jump and £1500 for his nap!' We used to have some fun and games with his napping. There's many a time I had problems with him; some days he would go and some days he just wouldn't. I remember one time going to Shrewsbury Flower Show; I rode into the ring and I went to go through the start and that was it. Maybe planted himself, glued himself to the floor. He just stood there, wouldn't go forwards, wouldn't go backwards, nothing. He never went through the start, I had to get off and lead him out.

We took the horse home and Ted had the idea of taking him hunting with the North Warwickshire. So Maybe became Ted's hunter during the week and my show jumper at weekends. That routine kept the horse fresh and got him going although we still had the occasional hiccup at shows, when he would nap again. He was a strange horse; when he went he was brilliant but when he didn't you couldn't move him at all.

I was now riding a few novices for Ted and Liz as well, in particular a big horse called Hello. He was a big 18-hand horse, and when riding him I looked like a pea on a drum. Steven Spielberg would have been proud of him, Hello would have been more at home in Jurassic Park. I remember one day in March at the Amberley Show he tripped up over an oxer and rolled all over me, he just rolled me into the ground. I looked like I'd been hit with a steamroller. He was a big useless yak.

Later the same day, Maybe came out and won the Young Riders class for me, which eased the pain of getting rolled on. With Maybe I was starting to win those red rosettes again like I used to back in the Oxo days and I started thinking that maybe show jumping isn't such a bad job after all. Ted was advising me to stay with show jumping and give up the idea of being a jockey and now that I was getting some success the idea started to appeal to me a bit more.

Maybe won a few other Young Riders Qualifiers and we were selected for the team to go to the 1974 Junior European Championships in Lucerne, Switzerland. We won the Team Silver Medal alongside Cheryl Walker with Wishbone, Lynne Chapman riding Mandalay Lass and Debbie Johnsey riding Assam. Debbie went on to finish fourth at the Montreal Olympic Games with Moxy; and I now see her most weekends as we have gone full circle and both our children are riding in the 12.2s. James Kernan won the Individual Gold Medal on a black mare called Marcella.

Ted was riding a horse called Everest Himself, a black Irish-bred gelding. I had been selected for the Junior Team at the Dublin Show. We went there with the horse and came home without him. Himself went so well for me that Eddie Macken saw him, tried him, liked him, bought him. But the horse wasn't so easy and I remember Eddie telling Ted a few years later, 'You forgot to send me the handbook when you sold me that horse!'

Wembley was always the last show of the season for us, so afterwards we were off for a winter of fox hunting. We used to travel the length and breadth of the country hunting with different packs and had a lot of good times.

I remember one day hunting with the Heythrop, hounds were running and we were flying, galloping up a field towards a hedge. Suddenly, David Tatlow, a very successful Point to Point rider and now leading Show rider, galloped alongside me, grabbed my stirrup and threw me out of the saddle. He thought it was hilarious! I was lying on my back in the middle of a spring barley field with everyone laughing at me. My horse galloped off up the field and I ran after it to catch it, thinking, 'Tatty, you'll pay for that one day.'

The opportunity came a couple of seasons later when David came to Edgars to try a hunter. Ted asked me to tack up the horse David was interested in and one for myself and take him off to jump a few typical hunt fences.

I led David around the farm, jumping hedges, ditches, gates, whatever we came across and on the way back I thought to myself, 'This is when I'm going to get him back.' On the farm there was an old pit, like a quarry. It lay in the Home Field (which was the jumping paddock) just behind a very high hedge. We usually avoided jumping the hedge into the Home Field at that point – the pit couldn't be seen from the take-off side and no horse had ever managed to stay on its feet when it landed. The drop was about 10 feet and the landing was on rising ground.

I set off up the field at a gallop, shouting over my shoulder to Tatty, 'I'll race you back home, make sure you follow me,' thinking, 'This is pay back time!' We went towards the hedge at a fair lick and I was calling, 'Straight on Tatty, straight on' and at the last moment I turned sharp right and pulled up. Tatty had nowhere to go but over the hedge and into the pit. As he left the floor I heard him shout, 'You bastard!' and sure enough he was up-ended.

When the horse got up he was lame and I got another bollocking from Ted but at least I had got my revenge. Tatty bought the horse after it had recovered! We still laugh about it now when we see each other. That was my motto in those days, don't get mad, get even!

Another time we had sold a horse to a guy up in Durham and we decided to deliver the horse and have a day hunting with the local pack, the Jedburgh, the next day. Alan Smith, a great hunting friend of Ted's was coming with us, so off we went with four horses – one each to hunt and one to sell.

We delivered the horse to the new owner and then arrived at our stables for the night at about five o'clock. I had to bed the horses down, feed, hay and water them and then we were out to the pub. As usual, I had to act as chauffeur, driving Ted and Alan home from the pub when they were half- pissed.

We woke up the next morning to find ourselves a foot deep in snow. That knocked the wind out of our sails; no chance of hunting in such deep snow. Then Ted had the brainwave of driving further north, away from the snow, to hunt with another pack. So we set off north to the Duke of Buccleugh.

Ted said to Alan, 'We'll put the kid in the back and he can plait them up on the way.' So I'm in the back of the horsebox as Ted dashes up north, we had to be there by 11 a.m. for the meet and it was a long drive. I remember being as sick as a dog in the back of that lorry. The road went up and down, up and down the hills, and I had the horses half-plaited and then had to stop to be sick. But it was worth it and we had a good day's hunting with the Duke of Buccleugh.

Afterwards, I had to do the horses off while they were in the pub. I used to have to do the horses first and then clean Ted and Alan's jackets and boots, as well as the tack. I never minded cleaning Ted's jacket because he was always at the front of the field so he didn't get very dirty. Ted was a brilliant man across country; I had great fun following him. Many a time we were sent home for taking our own line and being where we shouldn't have been. Sometimes we even arrived before the hounds.

On the way home the next day we stopped off at Carlisle and hunted with another pack. We had gone up the M1, across the country, and come back down the M6, a complete circle of the hunts.

We used to hunt at least three days a week in the winter and sometimes Liz would join us. We hunted the jumpers, something I don't do nowadays as the horses are so valuable, although I hunted Apollo and Major Wager once or twice.

Often we would not get home until seven o'clock at night because as soon as we finished hunting we would be in the pub, horses on the back of the wagon. One particular time there was a meet at Ted's place in Leek Wotton. Ted took great pleasure in getting everybody as drunk as possible before they set off. The meet took an hour longer than a normal meet. The punch was so strong … we used to empty the contents of the whole drinks' cabinet into the bowl, putting everything in it except petrol! Then Ted would watch everyone go down to the first hedge and enjoy the carnage. He didn't care how many rails they broke, he just liked watching the falls.

Afterwards, everyone would be back in the kitchen at the yard. I remember one evening, Brian Charlie, John Funnell and Dave Dick (Dicko) were in the house drinking. Their horses were all standing on their respective horseboxes out in the yard and I had a brainwave.

I went out and swapped Brian Charlie's horse with John Funnell's horse. When they came out, three sheets to the wind, they didn't notice and drove the horses home. The first person on the phone was Brian Charlie who went completely mad, he didn't see the funny side of it at all, he had a total sense of humour failure! After all, no harm had been done. John Funnell was OK about it – he figured that as long as he had a horse to hunt the next day he didn't care!

I had been riding a horse called Tycoon, an American-bred palomino. That horse really taught me to ride. If I wasn't right at a fence, it would stop and fire me on the deck. I soon learned to be right at a fence.

Ted decided we would take a team to the first-ever Team Chase that was going to be held at Hickstead – Douglas Bunn had the idea that Team Chasing would catch on, and he was right.

Ted rode Maybe, Bob Ellis had Sweet Charity, I took Tycoon, and Roland Fernyhough was on a point-to-pointer that looked as if it would leave the other horses standing. In a team chase it is the first three home that count for the time. Ted set off in the lead but Maybe knocked himself and had to be pulled up. I couldn't hold Tycoon and was having a complete memory loss about the course and Roland Fernyhough on his point-to-pointer was flying and gone for home. Tycoon was out on his legs, galloping blind, and the last thing I remember was he put both his front feet in a ditch toward at the last fence. We turned a somersault and I was left unconscious, underneath Tycoon who was also out cold.

Somebody dragged me out and I woke up in the ambulance tent. Ray Howe was holding his collarbone which he had broken in an earlier fall and there was this woman, crying her eyes out. She was bawling away, holding a lead and a collar with no dog in it.

It transpired that one of the King's Troop team horses had run out at a post and rail fence, jumped on top of the dog and killed it, stone dead. The St John's Ambulance officials had brought the dog's owner to the ambulance tent to calm her down a bit and console her. In the meantime, a marshall had picked the dog up, put it in a bin liner and slung it behind a Land Rover. Ray Howe was laughing his head off, he thought it was funny but the poor woman was completely hysterical.

I regained consciousness and I was taken to Cuckfield General Hospital where I spent four days under observation. The first of one of my very few holidays from Edgars. Every day, Carol Newton used to come to Cuckfield General and visit me. It was so thoughtful of her, it really brightened up my day.

CHAPTER SIX

European Champions

After the disastrous Team Chase at Hickstead, things started to improve. I was riding Maybe again now he had recovered from his injury; he was going well and winning consistently. Then a new horse with a hogged mane arrived from Belgium, his name was O.K.

Once again, Maybe was selected to represent Great Britain and we were in the team to go to the European Championships in Dornbirn, Austria. We joined John Brown riding Paddy Connelly and Marion Howard on Top Rank, Sally Mapleson with Waterbrook and Vicky Gascoine with Extra Special.

But then we had a little problem. Two days before we were due to leave, I was competing at the Royal Show in Stoneleigh when Maybe reverted to his old bad habits and decided not to take part. He flatly refused to go through the start. Embarrassingly, I had to get off and lead him out of the ring. Ted told Gerald Barnes, who was Chairman of the Selectors at that time, that Maybe wouldn't be going to Dornbirn but that I could take another horse, O.K. Gerald Barnes wasn't too pleased but it was too late to change the team – and Gerald wasn't about to argue with Ted anyway.

I was disappointed not to be taking Maybe as I knew it would be a real work of art to try and get O.K. to win a European Championship. He didn't have the best form in the world before going, only having won a couple of speed classes, that was all. And he wasn't the most careful of horses.

We set off to Dornbirn with all five horses in Sally Mapleson's horsebox, and all five of us young riders in there as well. It was bedlam. I had no groom and had to do my horse myself in those days, so I was really pleased that O.K. was hogged as I didn't have to plait!

When we arrived at the show I was in a very negative state of mind. I knew I had left my best chance of a medal back in Warwickshire eating grass in the paddock. It was August and the weather was very warm. Dornbirn was an outdoor show and the going was good. O.K. thought he was on holiday and was in a great frame of mind. He liked the sunshine and suddenly found his form.

Saturday dawned intensely hot, perfect for O.K. it seemed; it was the day of the Individual competition and I got up early in the morning to work him and give him a few jumps to sharpen him up. There were 67 starters in the Individual and instead of kicking the rails out as usual, he carefully tapped his way around, jumping by braille but leaving the fences standing. He astonished me by jumping clear, along with 21 others. In the second round we were clear again. By now I was beginning to feel a bit more confident. These two clear rounds put us into the jump-off against eight other riders. Guido Dominici produced the first clear round (tragically, Guido died from a brain tumour a couple of years ago and I was given the ride on his good horse Jalisco) but John Brown followed him in and tore round the course to take 6.7 seconds off him.

I was last to go and O.K. jumped the round of his life, fast and clear, to beat Daniella de Bruycker into second place by just under half a second leaving John Brown third with Paddy Connelly. O.K. and I were European Champions winning the Gold Medal! It was an amazing achievement for an average horse.

On the Sunday in the Team Competition, O.K. again jumped clear in the first round. The second round did not start for three hours by which time the weather had broken and it was pouring with rain. Lightning was flashing around the mountain tops and the surface of the grass arena (a football pitch in a former life) started to cut up badly. O.K. didn't like the weather change and had two down, which was more like his usual form. Marion and Top Rank were clear and four, Vicky had four and clear, and John Brown had four and four. Mine was the discard score in the second round.

The Gold Medal went to the team of four girls from Belgium, including Véronique Vastapane (later to marry Michael Whitaker),

Daniella de Bruycker, Hilda Goris (later married to Emile Hendrix, one of Holland's leading showjumpers today) and Marlene Marteens. We were equal second along with the Germans and the Polish who had shown remarkable form.

Ted's break becomes my lucky break

My big break came towards the end of 1977 when Ted broke his knee. Ted had a good string of horses and rather than just turn them away for a holiday while he was out of action, Ted gave me the ride on all of them. Now I was riding Lastic, Orchid, Jumbo, Louisianna and a few other good youngsters. With this team of horses, together with Maybe, I had as good a string as anyone in the country at that time. We were winning every week through out the county show circuit.

At the Town and Country Festival in Warwickshire that August I had a particularly good day. I won all three classes riding Lastic, Jumbo and Louisianna, a 17-hand German mare, big, scopey and very quick. In a big ring like that at Bath and West she was hard to beat. But she always had to go in a short-standing martingale as she carried her head very high. I was also doing quite well with Lastic; another German horse. Ted bought most of his horses from Germany in those days.

The county shows were good fun back in the 70s. We all stayed there together; it was like a holiday camp site. There were barbecues and parties in the stockmen's tent with all the farmers.

But Bath and West was always the best for after-hours entertainment. They had a big stockmen's tent there and they would always have a band on in the evening. There would be beer everywhere, farmers with their wellies on and a few old dears about.

I remember one night, outside the tent there was a hot-dog stand; a little stream ran though the showground and the hot-dog stand was next to it. One of the lads pulled an old bird who showed donkeys and went off with her. He took her behind the hot-dog van to have his way with her but without him knowing, the hot-dog van packed up and drove off, leaving him with his backside going up and down like a fiddlers elbow in full view of everyone, cheering him on!

With Ted side-lined by injury, he had more time than ever to keep an eye on my training. Some of his methods were not exactly orthodox. One time at Burley-on-the-Hill I was riding Maybe and Ted had put me in the Young Riders class. In the collecting ring he kept telling me I was sitting back over the fence when I was jumping. He wanted me to sit forward over the fence. I kept on jumping the practice fence but he wasn't satisfied with my position and suddenly shouted, 'Come here'.

Everyone always knew what Ted was up to because they could hear him shouting. He called me over to him and nagged, 'I keep telling you to sit forward,' and he got my tie and tied it to the martingale. 'That'll stop you sitting back,' he said.

Off I went, with my tie tied to the martingale and jumped the practice fence a few times. Luckily, I didn't have a fall and he untied my tie before I went into the ring. I got the point he was trying to make and sat forward after that.

The benefits of getting up early

Since winning the Junior European Championships, O.K. had maintained his form, showing flashes of brilliance every now and then. He had stopped kicking rails out all the time, now water jumps were his favourite thing to play with. He kept jumping in the water, he liked to paddle in them, not jump them.

At the Great Yorkshire Show that year we were entered for the Cock O' The North, which was the major championship at the show, and still is. We had competed there all week and the championship class was on the Thursday. For the last two days O.K. had jumped into the water, and as Thursday approached, I was thinking, 'How the hell can we clear the water, we have no chance.' Then Ted had the bright idea that we would get up as soon as it was light at four o'clock in the morning and school over the water. Along with Lol Weaver, Ted and I got up, tacked up O.K. and went down to the arena. Everything was asleep, cattle, everything. It was so still, you could have heard a pin drop.

At that time of the morning the gates to the arena were locked, so I jumped in over the hedge at one end of the arena. Lol and Ted built three or four poles into a triple bar over the water so the horse had to jump higher over the water rather than in it. O.K. soon got the hang of it and was jumping over the water nicely so we finished up and jumped back out. We were all walking back to the stables when a security guard came round the corner and saw us. We thought we were in trouble but then he said chattily, 'Can't beat an early start can you mate?' He was right!

We all went back to bed, but as we had been up at four we had a bit of a lie-in that morning and were half an hour or so late getting up. Ted was always first man up on the showground every morning so everyone else knew we must have been up earlier. They all presumed that they knew what we had been up to, as in the case in this game, everybody knows everybody else's business.

We walked the course for the Cock O' The North; there is an unusual feature in the class: there is always a double of six-foot-high walls. It is still a feature today. Anyway, getting up early didn't win us the class because O.K. knocked everything else down but cleared the water!

I kept the ride on Ted's string of horses longer than I had thought I would because he broke his knee again before it was healed. When he was first injured, the kneecap had been wired together and he came home with it all plastered from his ankle to his thigh. The first thing he did when he arrived was to get me to help him cut it off so he could get in the bath. We cut it in half lengthwise and kept the back half and bandaged it back on when he had finished his bath. Once it started to heal, he thought that now he was walking about a bit he might as well go down the field on his motorbike to get the sheep in. But he fell off it going through the gate and broke his knee again. So Ted was off injured for a long time.

Throughout the winter there was a Qualifying Circuit for the Lancia Final, which was held at Park Farm in Northwood, Middlesex. The final was three events in one day and the leading horse-and-rider combination won a Lancia car. Ted didn't own all of the horses I rode, we had owners who put horses with us but Ted would never stand any nonsense off owners.

NICK SKELTON ONLY FALLS AND HORSES

I was riding a horse called Orchid, one of Ted's string. We had qualified and went to the finals in the springtime. A man called Mr Wilkins owned Orchid. He had bought the horse from Ted for his son Robert to ride but the lad didn't get on with the horse; it didn't go for him at all. So Ted got the ride back and then it was passed to me.

The horse had won a few qualifiers with me and the owner was very excited about the horse going to the final because the horse had a good chance of winning. We got to Park Farm and it was a very cold day. The first class was a speed class and we got off to a good start by winning quite easily.

Mr Wilkins was very pleased and was thinking that now we'd won one class we were on our way. He was getting excited about winning the Lancia. But there was a long way to go, there were two more classes to be won. Mr Wilkins' excitement was starting to get up Ted's back. He liked to do, rather than talk about what he was going to do.

We had a break for lunch and the second class was a jump-off class and Orchid won again. Now Mr Wilkins was getting very excited, we were way out in front. He was nattering away to Ted, 'We're going to win the car, I can't wait to win the car, and when we get the car I'm gonna give it to my son Robert, he'll have the car,' and I could see Ted getting madder and madder.

Eventually Ted turned to me, 'This bloke's doing my head in, one more word from 'im and I'm gonna have 'im.'

Mr Wilkins then started telling Ted how to win the next class, 'Do this, do that,' and finally Ted turned on him and said, 'You won't win the car.' Mr Wilkins insisted, 'Yes we will.' But Ted said, 'I'm telling you, he won't win the car.' The bloke said emphatically, 'Yes he will,' whereupon Ted finally snapped. He snarled, 'He won't win the car, because you can take your fucking horse home with you. I'm sick of listening to you, and what you're going to do with this car!'

Ted was right, I didn't jump in the last class. He promptly told me to get the horse, adding, 'Don't give it a head collar, just get a bit of baler twine round it's neck. Tie it to the fence and leave it.' So I did as I was told and Mr Wilkins and his son Robert were last seen walking down the showground leading Orchid by a piece of string around its neck.

That same year, I returned to Austria for the first time since winning the Junior European Championships on my first Senior Nations Cup team in Laxenburg with Lastic and Maybe. It was my first trip abroad since the Junior European Championships win. Having Ted's string of horses to ride really was helping me make a name for myself.

CHAPTER SEVEN

Breaking the British High-Jump Record

At Olympia in 1978 there was to be an attempt to beat the British high-jump record. The record had stood for 41 years, and was held by Don Beard, riding Swank.

I was riding Lastic, and we won the Puissance, which was used as a warm-up class for the high-jump attempt. There were about ten of us trying for the record. It was late in the evening, the arena was packed, there was a full crowd in. The high-jump fence consisted of sloping poles, approximately 18ft long and bound round with rope, quite solid. It was built on a sloping wing, so it was quite wide from take off to the top rail.

We'd jumped from 6ft 6in up to about 7ft 3in, each time clearing it at the first attempt. When it came to the final round to break the record, Lastic had had enough. Out in the collecting ring Ted put up a big vertical, a single rail with a ground line. It was 5ft 6in or 5ft 8in and every time Lastic came down to it he ducked underneath the top rail, leaving me riding round the collecting ring carrying the rail on my arms. This is pretty dangerous, because hitting the rail at speed can break both your arms. We tried again, but again he ran underneath it. As preparation this was hopeless, so Ted put the fence down. Lastic couldn't run under it so he jumped it and in we went.

The fence in the ring was now standing at 7ft 7in 5/16th and as I rode in I was thinking there was absolutely no way we were going to be able to jump it. I came down for the first attempt and I didn't want to let him stop so I got a good bit of pace up; I had plenty of leg on and a good hold of him. Somewhere near the base of the jump he took off one too early and jumped straight into the middle of the fence. He broke two poles and had his legs everywhere, but he didn't tip up, he managed to land on all four.

I thought, 'Thank God for that. I've had enough of this, I can go out now,' and started to walk towards the gate. As I passed David Broome and Harvey Smith they both said, 'You wanna come out lad, you're gonna kill yourself.' I rode Lastic over to the gate but Ted wouldn't open it, he just leaned on it and told me, 'Don't take any notice of those two, get back in that ring and jump it.'

I wasn't in a position to argue (otherwise I would get another bollocking) so I started to canter up the side of the ring. I thought I needed a better stride this time and I came down and hit the take-off point just right. Lastic jumped it clear in front but just caught it behind and took the top pole off. He had hesitated a little on take-off but he had every right to hesitate! He had just crashed through it only a few minutes earlier. But this time he had bravely left the floor and just clipped it off behind.

Again, I walked towards the gate thinking, 'That's enough for now,' but Ted insisted, 'Get back in there and get it jumped. You're riding like a fairy.'

At that point I realised there was no way out; I was going to have to jump the damn fence. At least this was the last attempt and there was no way Ted could make me stay in that arena afterwards.

For the final attempt I turned my stick upside down, gave him one round his backside cantering up the side of the arena, got a good bit of rhythm and pace and I don't know whether the Lord was looking after me but I hit the right take-off spot. I remember looking down in mid-air as I'm at the top of the fence to see if everything was still intact. He did give it a bit of a rub behind but he didn't bring the rail down.

The whole arena erupted and went mad cheering. As I left the arena the crowd gave me a standing ovation, it was a terrific feeling.

Breaking the high-jump record was the first big stepping stone in my career, as it made my name. It was just a few days before my 21st birthday. Ted was pleased but wasn't giving me any of the £2,500 prize money – instead he told the newspapers that if I were lucky he'd give me a tie for Christmas!

I celebrated that night by going to Nicky Caine's 21st birthday party at her father's restaurant, Langans. I woke up with a real hangover the next morning.

They built the fence in the ring again the next morning and I had to go and pose next to it for all the press photographers.

I meet my future wife

Arena North was a fantastic outdoor show centre at Park Hall near Preston, up in Lancashire. It was situated at the side of the M6, and very easy to get to. They used to have three or four shows a year; it was a multi-level ring, with banks, water jumps, a lake, all on different levels. The whole thing was very picturesque and set in a bowl around which the seating rose like an amphitheatre. Sitting right up high you got a stunning view.

I remember one visit to Arena North especially. I was riding Wallaby who wasn't the easiest horse in the world as he was quite strong. We were through to the jump-off and they had built a fence just in front of a bank so that after the fence the horses had to jump up on to the bank, go around the lake and then jump back down and over a double of oxers.

I could see that it was possible to turn inside the lake, but it was very tight. I decided to jump the fence and then turn as short as possible, inside the lake – I tried it, turned inside and Wallaby took off again and jumped straight into the lake.

The lake had very steep sides and was quite deep and as he hit the floor he turned over. He was completely submerged and so was I. Ted was shouting at me to get back on and finish. For some reason I always used to do as I was told, so I sat on the bank, put my legs in the air to empty the water from my boots and got back on.

We set off towards the double of oxers but the saddle was so wet, my breeches were saturated, I couldn't hold the reins, couldn't sit in the saddle – I didn't stand a chance of staying on. Wallaby took off at the first oxer and being so wet I just fell straight off the back. I was on the floor again, to fits of laughter. It was a pity the round wasn't being televised because it would be good as a

Question of Sport 'What Happened Next?' clip. But then Wallaby galloped out of the ring and made his escape so I was able to walk out and get dried off.

Park Hall always had a good nightlife, there were some good nightclubs, and that night I went out with Geoff Billington. We were in the bar of a club having a drink, sitting telling a few tales, boys will be boys, that sort of thing, when we spotted Sarah Edwards and her friend Sian Cadwallader. Geoff pointed out, 'Them two are all right,' and we started chatting them up. As the evening wore on, Geoff ended up with Sian and I ended up with Sarah.

Afterwards, we went on seeing each other but Ted wasn't happy about me having a serious girlfriend because he maintained I should have no distractions in my life. He reckoned that you had to be 100 per cent dedicated. Added to which, Ted didn't really approve of Sarah, herself, because of her father Charlie Edwards. Charlie – a horse dealer – and Ted had fallen out several years earlier over a horse that had been sold. Charlie wasn't Ted's favourite person, so me dating his daughter didn't fit the bill.

Sarah was a good rider although her father sold all her decent horses because of his business. We got on well and later became engaged in March 1982. She was living up in Shropshire, Ellesmere, so at first I only saw her at shows. As the relationship progressed, I would drive up to Ellesmere on a Monday evening after work and take her out and then drive back the same night. It was quite tiring because I had to be back at the yard by 7 a.m. the next day.

In the end, I used to con my mate Greg Parsons (the chicken plucker) into coming with me and doing the driving. Sometimes we would get back at two o'clock in the morning, and then I would be up again driving over to Ted's to be at the yard for seven. I was still living at Odnaull End Farm. I never lived at the yard, so Ted didn't know what I was up to.

One time I was staying at my mother's and got back from Shropshire even later than usual. When I got up in the morning I was in a rush to get to work; I knew I was late and I didn't want to get the usual bollocking. It was a bit wet and misty that morning and I was tearing along a straight piece of road when suddenly I saw a half-timbered Morris Minor estate, parked on the road by the grass verge, with the bonnet up. With horror, I realised I was going too fast to stop and there wasn't room to overtake because of a car coming the other way.

Just before I collided with the Morris Minor I saw someone's backside sticking out from the side. I couldn't hit the oncoming car because I would have been wiped out. I had already hit the brakes and was screeching along, tyres squealing, when the fella with the Morris Minor heard me coming and jumped out from under the bonnet. But I couldn't stop in time, I hit his car up the backside, moving it several yards along the road and splintering the timber in the process.

I got out and inspected the damage to my car; the fan had gone through the radiator, my car was wrecked and I was thinking, 'Now I'm really late for work!' Miraculously, the Morris Minor started and I told the fella that I would get a bollocking if I didn't get to work so he gave me a lift to Leek Wootton. It was so good of him, in spite of the fact that I had crashed into his car, he took me to work! I left my car at the side of the road and was half an hour late but Ted didn't bollock me as much as usual because I had smashed my car up.

Ted had a strangely sadistic approach to cars. Like I have already said, he treated his own car as a dog kennel-cum-ashtray but he didn't have much respect for my cars either. One day I had to take Ted to Warwick where his cousin had an engineering company – he had been making something for Ted. We decided to take my car and as I was backing out of the place Ted said, 'I'll watch you back out,' and he did exactly that. He watched me back straight into a lamppost. He thought it was hilarious! That was in my good Capri, which especially annoyed me.

In those days I had bad car karma. Another time we were going to Warwick in the snow, Ted was with me and coming down to a junction in the road he said to me, 'You're going too fast.' I ignored him but when I put my foot on the brake to stop at the junction, sure enough I was going too fast for the road conditions. I slid on the snow all the way across the junction and straight into a garden wall and knocked it down. I was so mad, I had smashed up my third car within twelve months! I got out of my car and when the owner of the house came out I shouted at him, 'Why do you have to have a stone wall? Why can't you just have a hedge like your neighbour? Your wall's wrecked my car!'

Centre: Me at 18 months

Above: My very first pony

Top left: Riding Oxo in my cowboy outfit

Top right: Winning on the lead rein - Stuart
 Cruchlow on my left and Dad leading

Below: "Alka Zeltzer - First in the Fancy Dress -
 Mum in the background and Dad leading

Right: My dad when he was young

Top: 13.2's - riding Hanky Panky at Hickstead
Above: Prince Tarquin at Hickstead
Right: Filongley Show with Prince Tarquin - we
won the 13.2

Left: Maybe winning
the Whitbread Young
Riders Championship
at Wembley
Below: Dornbirn,
Austrian, 1975. O.K.
wins the Junior
European
Championships
Bottom: Himself at
Dublin Spring Show

Left: First attempt - How not to do it! See how I am stuck to him like glue. We didn't part company!

Below: Last attempt - How to do it! Breaking the British High Jump record at Olympia in 1978

Above: My wedding day - with my best man, John Whitaker
Top right: Signing my life away to Sarah!
Right: St. James winning the Du Maurier Grand Prix in Calgary in 1985
Below: Puissance at Dublin Indoor - calling a cab on Wallaby

Top: If Ever winning the Aachen Grand Prix
Above: J Nick at Hickstead
Right: With Sarah and Daniel after winning
the Derby with J Nick

Above: The team who won the European Championships in 1985 and 1987: l - r John Whitaker, Malcolm Pyrah, Ronnie Massarella, me and Michael Whitaker
Left: Apollo - Individual Bronze Medalist at St. Gallen in 1987
Below: Trotting up Apollo for the vet check at Seoul in 1988

Left: Riding Jappeloup in the
World Championships in
Aachen 1986
Above: The indoor stables at
Sandall House Farm. My
nephew Nicholas on the right
and my dog, Dora, walks off
refusing to be photographed!
Below: Sandall House Farm
after the renovations were
completed

CHAPTER EIGHT
The First World Cup Final

Volvo started the World Cup series in 1978 and as the qualifiers are held over the winter, the final is in the following year. By the end of my career I would have competed in sixteen World Cup Finals, a record only beaten by John Whitaker who has taken part in twenty.

I had been travelling around shows in Europe with Lastic and Maybe, but hadn't been to any World Cup shows. The last qualifier was in Geneva, shortly before the Final in Gothenburg. I was picked to go but my chances of qualifying were very slim. In those days the points system was different, you needed ten points to get to the final. I had no points at all. To get ten points I would have to win the Grand Prix.

Eddie Macken had a similar problem, he had to do well at Geneva, but he already had a couple of points.

As it happened, I won the Grand Prix on Lastic who was on form, and that gave me the ten points I needed. Eddie was second on Blossom Hill giving him eight points extra for a total of ten. Eddie had taken over the ride on Blossom Hill from Freddie Welch who went on to become one of my best owners.

I didn't think I had a chance, but it was a great challenge and I was keen to go to Gothenburg. I got a lift with Eddie in his horsebox and we drove up from Geneva, a very long way. I only had one horse, Lastic, so I looked after him myself.

All the top foreign riders were there including Americans I'd never seen before. Although the Americans only just made it there; the night before they were to leave the US to fly to Gothenburg, their aircraft – a Flying Tiger DC-8 – was stranded in Hanoi with engine trouble. There was a mad scramble to find another livestock cargo aircraft, and they landed in Gothenburg just in time.

The final ended with an exciting jump-off between Austrian Hugo Simon on Gladstone and Katie Monahan (now Prudent) on The Jones Boy. That was the beginning of a heated World Cup rivalry between the Americans and Europeans that dominated most of the 80s. Hugo's win was the only European victory in the first ten years of the World Cup and it wasn't until 1990, when John Whitaker had the first of his two wins with Milton, that the World Cup came back to Europe. Americans and Canadians won nine out of the first ten World Cup Finals.

I finished equal seventh with an American, Dennis Murphy. I felt this was another turning point in my career; I had broken the high-jump record with Lastic and had now been placed at my first World Cup Final.

Eddie Macken went really well with Blossom Hill to finish equal third with another American, Norman Dello Joio. The other British riders, Lionel Dunning and John Whitaker were equal fifth; Caroline Bradley was equal ninth with Germany's Peter Luther; Derek Ricketts and Harvey Smith also ran.

Sing along with Harvey

One time in Geneva, I had a run in with Harvey. We had been on the road in Europe for a few weeks along with David Broome, Harvey Smith, the late great Caroline Bradley, Derek Ricketts and myself.

Every night, after a show, we would always get Harvey singing. Harvey loved to sing, he was a great entertainer and after a couple of bottles of red wine he used to burst into song. He'd made a record at one time, called 'True Love'. His favourite song was Roger Whitaker's 'I'm Gonna Leave Old Durham Town' and every night he used to say, 'How's that song go?' He knew how it went, he just wanted prompting and egging on. We all knew the song and would usually give him the first couple of bars.

One evening we had been invited out to a house in Geneva for a dinner party and sure enough, after Harvey had consumed his compulsory two bottles of red wine he suddenly asked, 'How's that song go?'

David looked at me and I looked at him and we both raised our eyebrows: 'Here we go again,' I thought. So, me being young and with plenty of spring in me, I quietly said to David, 'I've had enough of listening to him.' The others were egging me on, 'Go on, tell him to shut up.'

I turned to Harvey and said, 'For God's sake Harvey, why don't you shut up, you know how the song goes.'

He looked at me and replied, 'If you don't shut up, I'm gonna take you outside and give you a slap.' With the bravado – or should I say stupidity – of youth, I said, 'Go on then.' So he got up, and I got up. I thought he was joking and everyone was laughing, they thought he was joking as well. We walked towards the front door and he went out first.

I followed him through and turned around to shut the door behind us. As I turned back to face him he punched me and the next thing I remember was waking up on the floor. He had knocked me out cold. With one punch. Harvey picked me up off the floor, dusted me down and said, 'Now whatever you do, we're not going to tell anyone, not Ronnie or anyone, we'll just tell them we came out for a bit of fun.' I thought, 'It might have been fun for him, but it wasn't for me.' We went back inside to join the others and I told no one until just now, when I told you.

The ups and downs of show jumping were proving to be a very steep learning curve. The moral is, if you're going to compete, make sure you can win!

A not-so-lucky break

Back home it was impossible for me to become big-headed, although I tried as hard as I could. Ted was always on my back. He used to shout at me, 'If you keep being late I'm gonna dock your wages!' But I would reply, 'I don't care, I don't do it for the money.'

Ted had a new horse, named Everest Granpa. He was a bit like Maybe, he had his own mind and was a nappy bastard. Some days he would go, and some days he wouldn't.

One day Ted was riding Granpa in the indoor school, having a fight with him. I was outside, filling up the lorry with diesel ready to go to a show when I heard Ted calling me, shouting, 'Come and help me with this horse!' When Ted said jump, you said how high? – There was no arguing with him. So I ran straight in there, I didn't even stop to switch off the diesel pouring into the lorry. Granpa was rearing up and napping and Ted told me to 'give him one with the long tom'. I picked up the lunge whip but didn't notice that it had been trodden on and was broken in half, so as I 'gave him one' round the backside I was standing much too close and when Granpa lashed out with both barrels he smashed my left hand.

I ran out of the school with blood pouring from my hand but I still had my wits about me; the first thing I did was run to the lorry and shut off the diesel. Then I was taken to hospital where they discovered I had broken three fingers, my thumb, and had a compound fracture of the left hand. And I'm left handed.

Another holiday … I was in Warwick Hospital for a week with my hand up in a frame at the side of the bed to keep it in shape and make it heal. After I came out of hospital I went straight back to work. That was the Edgar work ethic. Never mind that your hand was broken, as long as you had a hand you were expected to work. So I cleaned cars and did odd jobs, one-handed.

Meanwhile, Lastic was sold to Belgium and subsequently killed on a horse-walker. A dreadful end for a very brave horse.

The Moscow Olympics

The Olympic Games were scheduled to take place in Moscow in July of that year and Maybe was going really well. He was leading national horse and we were optimistic about a place on the Olympic Team. We didn't do any Nations Cups that year, we just stayed at home competing nationally but he had a lot of good form.

We were selected for Moscow but at the last minute we were asked by the government to boycott the games in protest against the Soviet invasion of Afghanistan. All the equestrian teams did as asked, but many of the British athletes went out there. One of the reasons we agreed to the boycott was because if there were trouble at the Games it would be very difficult to get the horses home. As it turned out a Polish rider won the Gold Medal, there being very little competition.

The FEI (Fédération Equestre Internationale) decided to hold an alternative Olympics in Rotterdam. Each different equestrian discipline had an 'alternative Olympics' at a different location. It was nothing like going to the Olympic Games but I didn't know that at the time. It wasn't until years later when I actually went to the Olympics that I realised Rotterdam was just another horse show.

I set off to the Netherlands with my fellow team members, Graham Fletcher riding Preachan, John Whitaker and Ryan's Son, and Tim Grubb riding Night Murmur, an American-bred horse owned by his wife Michelle.

When we walked the course for the Team competition I was staggered; it was absolutely huge, by far the biggest track I had ever seen or jumped in my life. I particularly remember the combination – an oxer, one stride that was a little bit long to a vertical and then two very short strides to a triple bar.

I was the first to go for our team, about sixth or seventh to go in the ring. So far, not a single horse had managed to jump the combination; five out of the first six fell at the triple bar because they were picking up off one long stride instead of taking two short ones. I was standing at the gate watching and thinking that I didn't mind about this. Maybe was good at taking two short strides, I always made him take extra strides as it was the best way for him to keep his jump.

Ronnie Massarella was standing with me as I waited at the gate; 'You don't have to go in if you don't want to,' he told me. But I replied, 'Don't worry, this horse'll jump round.' I went in and sure enough Maybe jumped the first clear round.

In the second round Maybe went clear again which meant we had jumped one of only three double clears in the competition, the others being Thomas Frühmann on a mare called Donau, and a Canadian, Mark Laskin, on Damuraz. Out of fifteen teams, I felt this was quite an achievement.

The British team finished up getting the Silver Medal. All the top teams were there, so we had beaten some good horses and riders. Only weaker teams had gone to the Olympics. We were just beaten by the Canadians who took the Gold Medal and the Austrians were behind us taking the Bronze Medal. Graham Fletcher went well, and so did John, but Tim Grubb's horse had stopped at the same fence in both rounds, although it was jumping unbelievable the rest of the time.

In the Individual competition Maybe had two down in the first round so I didn't go in the second as I had no chance of winning. John Whitaker and Ryan's Son jumped brilliantly – John took the Silver Medal, beaten again by the Austrian Hugo Simon, who won with Gladstone; Melanie Smith was third with Calypso.

The alternative Olympics were my first major senior championship and we had come home with a good result, I was pleased.

As usual with horses, no sooner was I up than I was back down again. A week later at Elms Farm, disaster struck.

Hickstead was scheduled to take place a week after Rotterdam and I had invited a couple of the American girls over to stay. Ted was OK about them staying at the yard with their horses, but my mind started to wander, losing that 100 per cent dedication to the job of show jumping which Ted considered so important.

The day after they arrived I took them hacking around the farm, turning on the charm, trying to woo them. On the way back to the yard we were riding through a field of loose horses when one galloped past me, lashing out with both hind legs. I heard a loud crack and felt a severe pain in my left leg.

Once again, off to Warwick Hospital where X-rays showed that I'd broken my leg. I actually had to take a week off work before being allowed back, on crutches, but able to do a few chores.

That loose horse certainly tried to put the mockers on my evil little plan!

Right place, right time

I was determined to get back in the saddle for the Horse of the Year Show at Wembley, which was in seven weeks' time. Lesley McNaught had joined the Edgars and the atmosphere at the yard had become very competitive.

I didn't miss Hickstead, I went to watch on my crutches. It was a classic case of every cloud has a silver lining, because if I had been riding, I wouldn't have been in the right place at the right time for what happened next. I was hobbling up between the Main Ring and Ring Two when a Rolls-Royce pulled up by the side of me. The guy driving wound the window down and asked, 'How are you doing with your leg?'

I told him I was getting along fine and then he went on to tell me that he wanted to buy a top horse for a top rider to ride. He asked me, 'Who do you suggest?' Well, I thought, that's a stupid question! I was hardly going to say, David Broome or Harvey Smith was I?

I told him I would ask Ted to get in touch with him; the guy was Terry Clemence. He drove off and I upped a gear on my crutches and went off to find Ted. He was in the top ring, about half a mile away, and when I had struggled up there I called to Ted, 'Hey! Terry Clemence just stopped me back there, he wants to buy a top horse for somebody to ride.'

Ted straight away replied, 'That's not a problem, I'll find him one.' Which he did. On behalf of Terry Clemence, Ted bought St James from David Broome but it was decided the horse should be ridden by Liz, not me.

My recovery was swift and I was able to ride at Wembley just seven weeks later. The first night back in the ring after breaking my leg I won the Butlins Championship with Maybe, beating John into second place with Ryan's Son, and David Broome into third with Queensway Philco.

CHAPTER NINE
There's Something in the Air

Having won the inaugural World Cup in 1979, the Americans were entitled to host the next final, but even though Baltimore boasted an ingenious Bert de Nemethy course, by all accounts I didn't miss much. Equestrian sports had limited appeal in the US back in those days and the show lacked razzamatazz. However, the result was a virtual American whitewash with six US riders in the top ten.

But Birmingham, close to my own home, was the chosen city for the 1980–81 final so I was very keen to qualify. I started my campaign at the Dublin indoor show in November where there was a World Cup Qualifier. I finished fourth giving me thirteen points towards the forty-five I needed to qualify. The rules had changed and ten points were no longer enough.

I ended the year at Olympia and then the horses took a well-earned rest for the next couple of months.

The first World Cup qualifying show in the New Year was Antwerp. It was the first show of the season as we had been resting up since Olympia. We had had two months off and were raring to go.

As usual I travelled with John Whitaker on Ted's lorry; John doing the driving because I didn't have an HGV licence. We set off on a six-week tour around Europe. In those days there was none of this nonsense of the riders flying from show to show, we all travelled together in the horsebox: two riders, six horses and two grooms in the back.

At Antwerp the show used to be held in the Sport Palais, which was located right underneath a motorway flyover, I think the motorway was the E40, Brussels to Rotterdam road. The horseboxes were parked directly underneath the flyover to provide some shelter. We arrived the night before the show but the hotel room was only booked from the following day, when the show actually started, so we had to stay that night in the horsebox and being a day early we had a free night. We were ready to let our hair down – we hadn't been let out for two months (!) and had to make up for lost time.

Off we went into the town, John and I, for a good night out. We met up with Kevin Bacon from Australia and a few others. As the night wore on we got on the Elephant beer; this is not your normal Heineken, it was the strongest beer they have in Belgium. We were quite fit but not really ready for this type of abuse to our bodies. We were like partly-fit horses - we blew up too early, we didn't make the distance! Having had a good lashing that night out on the town we made our way back to the lorries.

It was March, it was freezing cold, icy, minus temperatures. I was definitely in a better state than John; I had to half carry him back to the lorry. When we got there he sat on a hay bale outside the lorry saying, 'I don't feel so good, I'm going to sleep out here, outside the lorry.'

John has a very placid, quiet nature, but he can be headstrong at times. Once he gets his toes dug in he's very stubborn, more stubborn than a Blackpool donkey. And very determined. And he was determined to sleep outside on that bale. Finally, I lost my patience and dragged him into the lorry. If I had left him outside he would have frozen solid overnight. I got him up on to the mattress on the luton and clambered up beside him.

I clearly remember the clunking noise as lorries went over the motorway flyover above me. Clunk-clunk. Clunk-clunk. Clunk-clunk. Every two seconds, like a railway track. I thought it might keep me awake but the Elephant beer took over and I fell fast asleep. When I woke up in the morning I thought, 'Something smells funny in here.'

I was sniffing the air like a dog and I said, 'John, you all right?' But he didn't say a word. I turned over to look at him and saw what the smell was. He had been sick in the night. I thought, 'I don't believe this!' For a start he could have died, being sick in his sleep, but then I was worried about what Ted was going to say about John being sick in his lorry. I was wishing I had left him outside on the bale all night!

I got him showered and cleaned up and then we took all the sheets and mattresses down to the launderette before the boss got there, which we just managed to do. That was the end of the Elephant beer for that week! No more for us.

In the World Cup qualifier I got six points for eleventh place and John got eight points for thirteenth. Sunday night was the last night of the show and the next day we were due to move on to 's-Hertogenbosch. When the Grand Prix was over we went out and had another lashing but we didn't dare touch the Elephant again!

The following morning Malcolm Pyrah was trying to decide which one of us was sober enough to drive the lorry. He was quite a few years older than us and took his responsibilities seriously. John definitely wasn't sober enough, so I had to drive to 's-Hertogenbosch with no licence.

At 's-Hertogenbosch I was third in the qualifier earning 15 points. On we went with our European tour: Dortmund, Vienna and Gothenburg where we had a good run to finish up qualifying with 46 points. Once again, I had just scraped into the final.

While at Gothenburg I was watching the Puissance when I noticed a Belgian guy called Lionel Collard-Bovey riding a little strawberry roan, a French-bred horse by Nankin. It was tiny, only 15.3.

The horse had no mouth; Lionel had no control, nothing. In the Puissance, he went down the middle of the ring to a 5ft 9in square oxer with no control, and left the ground one stride too early. For whatever reason, the horse gave it a foot and landed a stride away on the other side. I thought, 'What a jump for a little horse.' He then turned around and galloped down to the wall at 6ft 6in and popped it just as easily.

I went outside and phoned Ted: 'I've just seen a horse here, it's a bit unruly but it can jump anything.' Ted was interested. 'But it's very small and very difficult.' Sure enough Ted got on to the people who owned it and he ended up buying it. The little roan was called

Epsom but after getting him home we changed his name to If Ever.

The World Cup Final for the 1980–81 season was held during April in Birmingham. Hall 7 of the National Exhibition Centre provided the setting for a very well-organised event, masterminded by the late Raymond Brooks-Ward. The event was televised to at least a dozen countries and over the five days there were 50,000 spectators.

I took Maybe and If Ever and was second to Franke Sloothaak on the opening day. On day two I crashed and burned picking up twenty-eighth place and we continued to fade after that, finishing in fourteenth place overall. Again, the Americans took six places in the top ten, although Harvey Smith and Malcolm Pyrah managed seventh and eighth, respectively.

On the Sunday, Liz had taken St James to his first show, the Heythrop Hunt Show at Richard Sumners showground in Chipping Norton. When she came to Birmingham to watch the World Cup that evening she told me, 'You've got yourself another horse, there's no way I can ride St James, he gives me a bad back every time he jumps.'

St James

I soon found out what it was that Liz found difficult about the way St James jumped. Whenever he jumped into a double or a combination he wouldn't land far out after each fence, he didn't make a lot of ground, so you were always a long way away from the second or third element. The good thing about St James was that he always made the ground up in his jump and had enough ability to pick up from wherever he was.

St James was a 16.1 liver chesnut, allegedly an Irish-bred thoroughbred type. A lot of people claimed to have bred him, but we never found out his true breeding. He was a difficult character, a nervous sort of a horse, especially in the stable.

And he was very difficult to get on. Literally. You couldn't just put your foot in the stirrup iron and get on him. I always made sure the groom had his saddle done up ready, rugs off, lead rope off, everything off, and then I used to plan my attack. I would walk up towards him and the groom would leg me up without me breaking stride, I would grab the martingale, reins, whatever I could, and off he would go. The minute your backside hit the saddle he was off, he started to canter straight away. After that you could rein him in and he would be fine and stand, walk, whatever. But you couldn't just get on and have him stand there.

St James actually used to jump off nervous energy; the busier you were on his back the better he jumped. The more adrenaline you had in you the better he went. He was a very, very careful horse. He didn't have the best technique in the world with his front legs, but he always tried to clear the jumps. And he was fast. I would say he was one of my all-time great horses. I wouldn't single him out as the best I ever had, but at that time there weren't many better horses around.

Over the years he had had a few different names; Fred Broome Sr first saw the horse at Bicton with Bina Ford at which time he was called Sunny Side Up. David Broome went to try him in Somerset in a small indoor school with ground that was six inches deep. David reportedly paid £5,250 for him and another £500 when he won his first class. The horse was bought for David to ride but he was a bit small for him, although they won sixteen classes together in one year.

Back then David was sponsored by Harris Carpets so Sunny Side Up was renamed Harris Homecare. That was the horse's name when Terry Clemence bought him. Terry told us that he owned the horse jointly with the owner of the St James Club in London so he was renamed again, St James.

My first time out with St James was at Amberley, which was the first big outdoor show of the season, held in Cirencester Park where the famous polo club is located. I was second to David Broome riding Heatwave in the Grand Prix. From being second at Amberley, the first big class St James won was the Grand Prix at Royal Windsor in the May of 1981, which he won for three consecutive years. After that, St James went on and won, won, won. He won the big classes at all the county shows: Surrey, Suffolk, Bath and West, South of England, Bucks, Royal Show, Kent. At Royal International in July he won nearly £10,000 winning the

Grand Prix and the John Player Trophy. That was good going by any standard.

Spruce Meadows

If Ever arrived at the yard and I started to jump outdoors with him. I rode him in a twisted wire bit, he really had no mouth at all and he would always run to the fence. Although he was only 15.3 he had an enormous jump. Ted used to work him and he would ride him every day for hours and hours, basically trying to put a mouth on him.

He gave him a lot of work on the flat. Ted was brilliant at working a horse on the flat. It's a knack, I don't think you can teach anybody how to do it. He had a special knack of working horses that it took me years to pick up. Another great master of working horses on the flat was Alwin Schockemöhle and I think Ted watched and learned from him. It took a long time to learn and it probably wasn't until after I left Edgars that I picked up what to do and how to do it properly.

Ted used to ride a lot of the horses, he would even work St James for me. It made my job easy, when I got on them after Ted; it was like driving a car with power steering instead of one without. The way Ted produced those good horses, like Maybe, St James and If Ever, I think he was ten years ahead of his time in working them. Ted's horses won so much at that time, they totally dominated the British scene in the early 80s.

In 1981, with all the horses going well, I went to Aachen, which is the mecca of European show jumping. I rode on the winning Nations Cup Team with Maybe, along with Liz on Everest Forever, Malcolm Pyrah with Towerlands Anglezarke, and Fred Welch (my owner-to-be) on a grey mare, Norstar.

The following week I went to Dublin with St James and rode him in the Nations Cup and then we flew to Spruce Meadows in Calgary for the first time ever. St James travelled on the livestock transporter, and I flew separately on a passenger aircraft. St James had never flown before but he coped well and arrived in good shape.

I hadn't been to any of the North American horse shows and when I arrived my first impression was that Spruce Meadows was just a big field, with a ring, one building at the side of the ring where the judges sat, and the secretary's office.

That is all it was. There was no indication of Ron and Marg Southern's hidden agenda that Spruce Meadows would grow to be the biggest horse show in North America, attracting crowds of nearly 200,000 throughout the show and covering 315 acres of prime Alberta farmland.

On Saturday and Sunday a few local folk turned up to watch and there was a bit of a crowd there. Why had we come all this way? Because the Grand Prix had a huge first prize, $30,000, that was the reason we all went. If I remember rightly, I think David actually won the Grand Prix on Philco.

In those days the showground was way out of town in the sticks, quite different to how it is today. Calgary has grown out of all recognition, the suburbs slowly encroaching on the land towards Spruce Meadows. Nowadays Spruce Meadows probably ranks with Aachen as one of the top horse shows in the world, offering fantastic prize money, $250,000 to the winner of the Grand Prix, watched by upwards of 60,000 people in stands and sponsors' boxes which provide every possible comfort. It is phenomenal.

Every year I have gone back, something has improved and nowadays Ron and Marg Southern run it along with their two daughters, Linda and Nancy, both good showjumping riders.

On that first visit, I was impressed by their hospitality and this has never changed over the years. They always make you feel so welcome, anything you need doing, nothing is too much trouble, they are so helpful; they are brilliant show organisers. Ron Southern wanted to build Spruce Meadows into one of the greatest showjumping venues in the world, and he has realised his dream.

CHAPTER TEN
I Lose St James

Terry Clemence's daughter, Sarah-Jane, had ridden successfully in ponies and now she was seventeen she wanted a Young Riders' horse. Over the winter it turned out that she had her eye on her father's horse, St James. She knew that a top horse like St James would give her the best possible chance of making the Young Riders team.

Blood being thicker than water, under protest from both Ted and me, we had to give the horse up to Sarah-Jane to ride and she took St James home to Epping in Essex.

She started riding him in March and, in all fairness, come the beginning of the outdoor season she was going quite well, winning seconds, thirds, Young Riders' classes, that sort of thing. But then St James started to have the odd stop. Horses like St James that are very, very careful over a fence, don't put up with too much nonsense over missing them and messing them about. So he kept having the odd stop.

In the meanwhile, I was riding If Ever who sticks in my mind as a good horse but, in fact, only ever won five classes with me. However, If Ever was all I had, so I had to focus on him as my top horse. He got off to a good start by winning at the May Hickstead meeting; in the Grand Prix I was equal first with David Broome on a horse called Mr Ross – we dead-heated to share the prize money of £9,500.

Then I went off with If Ever to Lucerne on the team with Liz who was riding Forever, Malcolm Pyrah on Chainbridge, and Pam Dunning on Roscoe. It was my first time abroad with If Ever and the weather was awful, it rained all the time. In the first round I had

24 faults and Liz was clear. Then in the second round Liz had 24 faults and I was clear! So, no disgrace there! We accumulated 48 faults between the two us but the team was able to discard the cricket score in each round.

Back home I read the Lucerne write-up in Horse and Hound; Pam Dunning had written the article under a ghost name and was blatantly biased in her reporting. She wrote about how badly Nick and Liz had done, but emphasised how brilliant Pam Dunning was to jump a double clear on Roscoe and take the team to win!

From Lucerne our European tour took us to Aachen. In those days the Aachen Grand Prix was run over four rounds; two complete rounds, then a Puissance round of eight big fences and after that all the clears went against the clock in the final round. In 1983 the Grand Prix was changed to three rounds.

The rain had followed us from Lucerne, but now it was torrential. The Grand Prix was a gruelling course and it was entirely down to If Ever's temperament and strength, and how brave and tough he was that he kept going throughout the four rounds. His stamina saw him through, which was due to Ted's work on the flat, hour after hour.

In the final jump-off If Ever took a second off Flambeau II and Frédéric Cottier; then Hugo Simon on Gladstone completely mistimed the second to last fence and Paul Schockemöhle took Deister too short to the wall, making me the third consecutive British rider to win the Aachen Grand Prix, one of showjumping's toughest competitions. I now had a chance of going to the World Championships in Dublin in August.

Back in England, we went to the July Hickstead meeting. In the Grand Prix at Hickstead they had a very wide fence; the actual poles were 10ft long, and on either side there were two walls that were very narrow, about 3ft wide. The flags were on the outside of the walls, so in effect the walls were part of the jumpable part of the fence.

Whenever I held If Ever he would cock his jaw and run right-handed and that's what he did that day. He had actually run out at the fence but at the last minute I managed to haul him back in and got him to jump the narrow wall, just inside the flag. We won the

Grand Prix and £8,000. If Ever was on a roll.

During Hickstead the team was picked for the World Championships to be held later that year in Dublin. I was picked with If Ever as non-travelling reserve and the four on the team were Malcolm and Anglezarke, John and Ryan's Son, David with Mr Ross and Pam Dunning with Roscoe.

Then tragedy struck and the New Zealand-bred Roscoe broke his leg when he fell at the dry ditch by the Derby Bank and had to be put down. As reserve I was automatically put into the team.

The next bit of luck I had was at the same meeting; Sarah-Jane Clemence was riding St James in the main ring in the Young Riders' Championship and I can still see him now – there were three verticals in a combination going towards the lake and he stopped and was eliminated.

After that, Sarah-Jane finally said she couldn't manage the horse, she thought she would ruin it. She dismounted and generously gave him back to me. We actually took St James back home from Hickstead a few days later.

World Championships

Then it was off to Dublin for the World Championships with If Ever. Well, what a disaster this turned out to be, although the team did win a bronze medal.

The course for the Nations Cup sticks out vividly in my memory; I walked it with Malcolm Pyrah. We strode the distance from a wall, which was on a dog-leg of five-and-a-half strides, to a pretty big double of oxers. We had the choice of five forward strides or six short. Malcolm said to me, 'Oh well, jump the wall and then its five strides forward because the oxers are too big, you'll have to go forwards to jump these oxers.'

But what Malcolm didn't take into consideration was that his horse always jumped slightly to the right - whereas my horse always jumped to the left. Malcolm was walking the course for Anglezarke, not If Ever, and I was listening carefully, taking advice and thinking, 'I'll pay attention to a more experienced rider.'

So, I automatically took his advice and thought, 'Oh well, five strides for me.'

I was first rider in for the team and the wall was fence five or six. As I went round I remembered Malcolm's words, 'Five strides forward to the oxers.'

As usual, my horse jumped to the left over the wall and I set off for five strides on the dog-leg to the big oxers, counting, 'one-two-three-four-five' … When I got there I was a mile off but I still gave If Ever a big kick and expected him to pick up, but there was no way he could do it. He stopped, slid down on to his backside like a dog, obliterated the fence and I fell off.

I got back on, the arena party rebuilt the fence, then I jumped the double of oxers, turned right-handed and continued to knock down another three fences. We had lost all our rhythm, concentration, everything.

We turned back left-handed towards the entrance and there was a gate; If Ever stuck his head in the air and just ran at the gate, I was fighting him to try and keep him under control, but we ended up hitting the gate, whereupon he stopped, sat down and I fell off again!

I climbed back on again, and continued to finish the course. With time faults, I ended up with 56 faults. Not bad for my first World Championship!

When I left the ring I continued to blame Pyrah for telling me to go on five strides but it was my own fault really. From that day on I learned an important lesson; make your own mind up for the horse you are riding, walk the course for your own horse and not somebody else's.

In the second round we made an incredible recovery and finished with only four faults, having just the last fence down, otherwise I would have jumped a clear round. Amazingly, our team ended up with the bronze medal.

Malcolm went on to win the silver medal in the Individual. It was the funniest thing watching Malcolm riding Fire, Norbert Koof's horse, which was 18 hands high – Malcolm looked like a pea on a drum, he's only about 5ft 6ft.

After our disaster at Dublin we went back to Hickstead where If Ever won his fourth Grand Prix in succession that same year.

Coming up to the World Cup final that spring, John and I were first and second in the European league, John just pipped me for first place as European league winner. At Gothenburg, the last qualifier before the World Cup Final in Vienna, If Ever won the Grand Prix taking his total tally with me to five. That was it. He only won five classes for me the whole time I rode him.

Of course, I didn't know that was the last class he would win for me so off I went, feeling quite confident, to the World Cup Final in Vienna along with Malcolm, David, Steven Hadley and Liz.

I took St James as well as If Ever, but had a bad first day, a bad second day, and then a good last day which brought me up the placings. I had ridden St James in first leg, which was a disaster, and then jumped if Ever in the next two legs, ending up equal first in the third leg with John Cottle from New Zealand riding Arturo and Norman Dello Joio who won the final with I Love You. I finished up sixteenth overall, equal with Stephen Hadley and Sunorra.

But for personal reasons, the show was a nightmare.

On the morning of the second day, having a had a bad day the previous day with St James, I was in my hotel bedroom when Sarah telephoned to tell me that Stuart Crutchlow, my best friend from earlier days and one of the 'three musketeers' had been killed in a car crash the night before. He was in the car on his own and simply drove off the road and crashed into a tree stump.

It was an appalling tragedy, especially for his wife Cheryl and his young lad, Nick, who had been named after me. Stuart's lad is now twenty and I see him quite often. He is absolutely the spitting image of his dad.

CHAPTER ELEVEN

Just Married

Back in March of 1982 I had got engaged to Sarah Edwards. We were getting serious, thinking about settling down, so we got engaged. This didn't go down at all well with Ted, who liked complete control and total concentration; he thought my relationship with Sarah would take my mind off the job.

We were supposed to get married in September but Sarah called the wedding off and we didn't get married until October.

I had started to think that I was not only invincible, but invisible. All this winning had gone to my head; the success, nights out, I would have a few drinks to celebrate, and then I would think I had become invisible. Anyway, I got led astray (like my old headmaster used to say, 'Nick was very easily led') and I was seen out with another girl.

My crime was reported to Sarah and she called off the wedding and came round to the house and took all her furniture away. But after a lot of effort on my part she forgave me and in October we were married in Solihull Registry Office followed by a riotous reception at the Balsall Common Equestrian Centre, the scene of so many of my youthful escapades.

Our first home was Oak Cottage at Beausale, a couple of miles from Edgars' yard. It was a really quaint little cottage, with low beams and about an acre of paddock. I built three or four stables for Sarah so she could have her horses there.

We had to do some renovations, replacing the bathroom and the kitchen but it was in good nick, generally. I had been living at Odnaull End Farm with my father and this was the first time I had lived away from home. Sarah moved down from Shropshire where she had been living with her parents and brought a few horses with her so she could bring on youngsters and do a bit of dealing. The acre of paddock had to double as an arena as well as a turnout field – Sarah had to make do with a couple of jumps in the paddock and road work.

I was in the middle of a busy show jumping schedule so our honeymoon was a trip to Amsterdam for a show. As usual, John Whitaker drove Ted's lorry but now we both had wives with us – John had married Clare a while back, and Sarah and I were 'Just Married!'

As we drove out of the docks at the Hook of Holland we looked at the diesel gauge; John and I decided we thought we had enough to get us to the show but we were wrong ... and sure enough we ran out of diesel. Stranded on the side of the motorway, we started getting a lot of verbal abuse from the women who had suddenly become expert mechanics, or so they thought. They kept telling us what we should have done, what we shouldn't have done, how we should bleed the engine.

John and I had soon had enough of this abuse so we left them and walked to a fuel station that we could see along the road and bought a can of diesel. The problem then was how to get the diesel out of the can and into the tank. We didn't have a funnel and the diesel cap was well underneath the lorry, all we had was a plastic can. Then John had a bright idea and he fetched the hollow aluminium table leg out of the living area. We stuck that into the tank and poured the diesel down the leg of the table. It worked a treat as a funnel!

Then, of course, we had to bleed the engine, which is where the women really came into their element, but despite their constant (and useless) interfering, John and I succeeded in getting the engine started and we drove down the road, filled up with diesel and went to Amsterdam for the show.

Not much of a honeymoon! And not a good start to a marriage.

Friction

Back at work after the honeymoon, the atmosphere slowly started to change and the rot set in.

I was now a married man with responsibilities, bills to pay, the days of earning a pittance were long gone. Things were very different. I went home at lunchtime, which was unheard of, and reappeared afterwards. And of course I was no longer 100 per cent under Ted's influence. I was in love with Sarah and she was a big influence on my life on a daily basis. I was still as committed to winning as before but Ted no longer had total control of me, which he resented; he thought my mind was wandering.

Friction arose between Ted and me. I was no longer Ted's gofer; I was no longer always at the yard. Oak Cottage needed my input and what with building the stables and making all the improvements, I had other things to think about. Lesley McNaught's presence at the yard also started to cause problems. Ted started giving more of his attention to training Lesley who lived at the yard full time, which allowed him to have total control and influence over her.

Over a long period of time, the relationship between Ted and me slowly started to split apart. Lesley was now the up-and-coming stable jockey, she was riding more, winning more, she won a European Junior Championship with One More Time and became very successful.

With Liz, Lesley and me riding, there were a lot of jockeys for the horses to go round. The rift in the Everest Team slowly became more apparent and I started to go to shows with Liz while Ted took Lesley under his wing and we ended up going to different shows.

Going to shows with Liz turned out to be good for me. She helped me when the job of show jumping became technical as courses changed over the years, and Liz was one of the first people to work out how to stride the related distances between the fences and how to judge the distances.

Liz was, and still is, one of the best show jumping riders; even today, she is a fantastic person to watch and learn from. She was a brilliant rider and a big influence on my career. Liz won a lot of good classes and if she had had a really good horse like Milton or Jappeloup, she could have been European Champion, World Champion or Olympic Champion, as she was good enough to ride at the highest level.

Slowly, it became like a team competition within the Everest Team. Who did best on the day became the topic of conversation. If we all ended up at the same show and I didn't go so well, Ted would give me another bollocking. He was also tough on Lesley, but she was a girl so he did treat her in a slightly different way.

Lesley had broken into the big league and one day Ted decided that she would do better on a horse called Barbarella than I had been doing. To be fair the horse had been going well for me but then simply lost a bit of form. But Ted saw his chance and took the horse off me and gave the ride to Lesley.

It got to the point where I felt I had to protect Apollo and St James. If either of those horses were being left at home for a rest, I would load them on to the horsebox and take them to the show, just for a day out. I was scared to leave St James at the yard because if something had gone wrong I wouldn't have put it past Ted to have given the ride to Lesley McNaught. Although in the end, I outlasted her by two-and-a-half years.

CHAPTER TWELVE
The Fall Circuit

My second trip to North America was to Washington, New York and Toronto. The Americans call this the Fall Circuit because it's in the autumn.

I took St James and a chesnut mare named Arabesque; I didn't have any team-mates with me, I was competing as an individual. The horses, cared for by Lisa Barnes, flew on ahead of me in a livestock transporter but as I left England on British Airways I thought, 'Well at least I've got my best horse with me, Ted can't take him off me while I'm gone!'

At Washington I had a really bad show and didn't win anything. It was a seven-day show, which is quite a long time and every day I drew a blank. St James was competing in the bigger classes as he was my best horse but being very, very careful he was unhappy trying to cope with the American courses, where the fences were wider and the distances longer than he was used to.

Here in England, the distance in a one-stride combination would be eight yards whereas in America it was eight-and-a-half yards. And a two-stride double would be eleven-and-a-half yards in England, but in America they would give you twelve-and-a-half yards. It was the same with the related distances: four strides should be twenty yards, but over in America you would be given twenty-one yards. This meant you were always going forward to the fence. And yet the distance would be too short to put in an extra stride. The Americans were riding forward-going thoroughbred blood horses and the courses suited them, but I was always riding with my foot to the boards.

In addition to the distances being too long for St James, the poles were much heavier, the fences more solid with fillers, unlike the light, airy English fences. So when he did hit a pole, which he hated doing, he wasn't happy.

Each of the seven days, I was calling back to the yard to report that I hadn't won anything and it was starting to annoy Ted. Arabesque won a bit, but not much and by the end of the show, with no big win, Ted was not in a very good mood.

We moved on to the six-day New York show where I hoped my luck would change.

The show was held on the third floor of Madison Square Garden. Stabling was up on the third floor and the horses had to be walked up a ramp, like in a multi-storey car park. The ceilings were very low and it was extremely hot for the horses. In the stable area the tannoy kept repeating, every two minutes, night and day, 'Please extinguish all smoking materials by order of the New York City Fire Commission.' It drove us all completely mad.

Also, it was difficult to exercise your horse, you couldn't just go out and do road work – you were on Seventh Avenue! There was a rota system for exercising, and sometimes 4 a.m. would be your allocated time. Jumpers, Hunters, High-Steppers (which we call Hackneys), Tennessee Walking Horses; they were all allocated different times to exercise before the show started each day. Competitions started at nine o'clock in the morning, although the show jumping never took place until six or seven at night. You couldn't swing a cat around in the collecting ring and there were two pillars in it as well, which didn't help matters. The main ring was oval and very small.

After the first day's jumping I drew yet another blank. Now it was agony phoning home and having to report back. It was painful. I was starting to hold the phone at arms length so I didn't have to listen to the barrage of abuse down the line from England: how Ted had sent me all the way to American, at vast expense; but that I was so useless I couldn't win anything.

Then all of a sudden, on the Friday, without any warning, I was warming up for a class and across the collecting ring I spotted Ted. He came storming across and started roaring at me, so loud that everyone else could hear. The collecting ring was so tiny, they were well within earshot. He was giving out at me just like on the phone, but now he had an audience. He was telling me I was useless, he just kept going on about how hopeless I was until my patience snapped and I turned to him and said, 'Why don't you fuck off back home?' At which he turned around and left and I never saw him again, I assume he flew back to England.

I thought I'd better get a different plan. Again, St James couldn't manage the distances in New York so I decided the only thing I could do was to try Arabesque in the bigger classes and use St James as my speed horse. Arabesque had a bigger stride, she was scopey, she would cope better with the wide fences and the long distances where as St James had no chance. So that was the plan, swap them round for the Grand Prix on Sunday.

As it happens, someone up there was looking out for me and Arabesque won the Grand Prix. Now I was only too pleased to pick up the phone and call home, but I had to tell Liz that I had won, I was not in Ted's good books. Liz was delighted and she went and told Ted who was not exactly speaking to me. St James didn't like the speed classes, the damage was already done, I had him all strung out trying to get the distances but he clearly didn't like America. America was not for him.

New York was a very sophisticated show. For the evening performances everyone dressed up like I had never seen. Men would come in top hat and tails, the women came loaded down with jewellery in evening dresses. And every night, at about eleven o'clock, after the show finished, there would be unbelievable parties on the top floor of the New York Penta across the street on Seventh Avenue. Bands, food, dancing and as much drink as you wanted. They were fantastic evenings. Then after the party it was back to the stadium to exercise your horses if you had an early slot in the rota.

On a trip to New York a few years later, John Whitaker turned up one morning straight from the party, still wearing his evening suit. Everyone else had changed into boots and chaps, but not John. He just got on and exercised his horses in the arena and then went off to bed for the day.

I think it was on that same Fall trip, in Toronto, that John and I were there for seven days and never saw daylight. We jumped all evening, partied all night, and slept all day.

In those days we had the best chauffeur in the world because the Hungarian rider Joe Turi never partied. So when we finished jumping at midnight we would get Joe to take us to the parties and on to the nightclubs. And then we would emerge at four, five o'clock in the morning, go to the stadium and exercise our horses from six until seven and then go to bed before it was light. Then the next day we would do it all over again. It was like being on British time!

Enough about parties. Next stop was Toronto, which was a ten-day show. It was the Royal Winter Fair and there was an awful lot going on, cattle, sheep, you name it. A huge agricultural show.

I arrived in Toronto and I was amazed when the first person I saw was Alan Oliver, an English course builder. Alan used to ride himself and had some good horses years ago. I asked him what he was doing there, and he told me that he was building the courses. I was so relieved and told him, 'St James is going to be glad to see you,' and explained that the American distances hadn't been doing him any favours. 'I hope you are going to build in your style, not theirs,' I suggested optimistically.

He replied, 'Definitely.'

From then on St James was a different horse and changed completely, he was back to his old self. He won two big classes and ended up winning the Grand Prix over good old-fashioned English courses! St James loved Canada but he still hated America. I went home having redeemed myself and in time Ted forgave me for swearing at him. But he didn't forget, he only forgave.

St James flew home and at Olympia that year he won the Grand Prix and the World Cup, so no harm had been done by those long American distances.

Apollo

Geoff Glazzard had been riding a horse called Apollo for owner Linda Jones. Apollo was a white-faced Dutch-bred 17-hand gelding by Erdball and Linda had bought the horse in Holland for her nephew to ride. However, it proved too difficult and she took it along to Steve Hadley for some help. The horse was stopping really badly, but Steve was moving house at the time and instead of taking the ride himself he suggested she send it to Geoff Glazzard who lived up her way in Staffordshire.

Geoff got Apollo going really well, winning a lot with him and to this day I still don't know how we ended up getting the horse. Geoff Glazzard won three or four big classes with him at Wembley, the horse wasn't going badly, but all of a sudden Apollo appeared at our yard.

Thankfully. Because he ended up being a fantastic horse for me, definitely one of my great horses.

He could win the fastest Speed Class, the biggest Grand Prix and he would eventually jump 7ft 5in in the Puissance at New York. He won two Grand Prix at Aachen in 1987 and '88, two Dublin Grand Prix in 1988 and '89, an Individual Bronze Medal at the European Championships in St Gallen, and Bronze at the World Championships in '86. To top it off he won the Grand Prix in New York and Toronto in '86, two consecutive Hickstead Derbys and was second three times, and he won the Speed Grand Prix in Calgary by five seconds, plus many more classes.

The first class I rode him in was at the Royal Show here in Warwickshire. Apollo used to jump to the left so I put a small brush on the inside of the bit, on the left, to help him keep straight. I went in the main ring at the Royal, jumped the first fence and he bolted with me. He didn't like that brush at all. We did two laps of the arena before I was able to pull up and come out. That was the end of the brush idea.

Apollo was an awkward character. He was quite a nervous horse and again, like St James, he was difficult to get on. I always had to get the rug taken off first because if you got on and then took the rug off his quarters he would bolt.

Also, turning him out was nerve-racking. If he knew he was going out in the field, as he came out of the stable he would just gallop down the yard to the paddock. Then he was fine. Just stood and grazed. He was very clever, and knew the difference between an indoor rug and an outdoor rug. If he had his New Zealand rug on, as soon as the stable door was opened, he would charge off down the concrete, there was no way of holding on to the head collar and rope. After a while, we gave up trying and just opened the field gate and then opened the stable door and let him get on with it.

Apollo was brilliant for the big occasion, a real showman. The bigger the occasion, the better he went. You could always bring him out after the winter break and go straight to a big show. He didn't need a warm up. I could take him straight to a top show like Rome and almost guarantee he would win the first class. He often did.

I wasn't allowed to go to the 1984 Olympics because I had turned professional when I was sponsored by Everest and in those days a sponsored rider was classified as being professional. So the 1984 team of John Whitaker and Michael Whitaker, Tim Grubb, and Steven Smith (younger brother of Robert Smith), went off to Los Angeles where Tim Grubb redeemed himself and the team won Olympic Silver Medal. Steven later suffered a dreadful motorbike accident that severely damaged one arm and finished his show jumping career.

That year, Ted was training the Australian team who were based in Stow-on-the-Wold at the late Laurie Connell's. Laurie owned the horses ridden by Jeff McVean (one of the Australian team) and being about the same age we struck up a good relationship and became very good friends. He did well here in Europe with a horse called Furst Z and we had a lot of very good times. I was sorry when he returned to New Zealand in 1989 and I hadn't seen him again until earlier this year when he came to visit me with his wife Vicky and his two daughters, Kate and Emily, who came to stay with me last year.

Laurie Connell had racehorses in training with David Nicholson who was based nearby in Gloucestershire. One New Year's Eve, Jeff and Vicky had a party at their house and I was there with John and Michael Whitaker and David Nicholson. As the evening wore on, somebody suggested that it would be a good idea to get up very early the following morning and go and ride out at David Nicholson's. David didn't think there was a problem, but told us to be sure to be there at seven o'clock in the morning.

Well, we didn't go to bed until about three and both the Whitakers are very good sleepers, so I knew it was going to be difficult to wake them up but sure enough I woke up at half past six.

I looked out of the window to see torrential rain and began to think that maybe this wasn't such a good idea after all but I knew we couldn't let David down as he would have four horses tacked up for us that morning, waiting. Only Michael and I got there – David was surprised to see any of us I think! He didn't think I looked well enough to ride, but I managed. Michael rode What A Buck up over the steeplechase fences and made a good job of it, he took to it like a natural. Michael would have made a good jockey. On that cold, wet morning, with no indoor school, I realised I'd made the right decision not to be a jockey when I'd taken up show jumping instead!

CHAPTER THRIRTEEN
My First Son is Born

In August 1984, Sarah fell pregnant. We had been married two years and it was good timing. She went on riding for a while until she became too heavily pregnant to cope.

The pregnancy was another nail in the coffin for Ted and me. He didn't seem to approve of me having children and I remember one comment he made which upset Sarah.

We were all packed and loaded up to go to the Horse of the Year Show and Sarah was coming with me in the horsebox. When Ted came out of the house and saw her in the passenger seat he said to her, 'Haven't you got anything better to do?' This really upset Sarah. She was already several months' pregnant and all she wanted was to come to the show. Ted clearly wasn't in the best of humours and I thought, 'Oh, this is the start of a good week,' as we set off to the show.

On the first day, Monday, I drew a blank and won nothing. Tuesday was the same. Wednesday, blank. The show was turning out to be another disaster, just like the American Fall Circuit. Ted's mood was not very good as you can imagine and I felt he was blaming my marriage for my lack of success. Then on the Thursday I had a change of luck. Halo pulled out and won the Grade B final and from then on I started winning. I went on to win all four classes on Thursday, all four on Friday and two more on Saturday.

Ted's mood had now improved.

The last class on Saturday night was the Grand Prix. St James was clear in the first round and last to go in the jump-off. I was going for win number eleven. We were clear to the last and I made the fatal mistake of thinking I was home. I was a little bit too far off the last oxer and he just clipped it behind.

The eleventh class was not to be. We finished third with the fastest four faults. To be fast and clear and then knock the last fence down, that is unforgivable. And nine times out of ten it is the rider's fault. You're anxious, you're going too quick, and bang, the last fence comes down.

Despite winning ten classes on the trot, Ted bollocked me all the way home up the M40 about the eleventh class. I just sat there, at one o'clock in the morning, taking all this abuse, thinking, 'What do I have to do to please him?'

A left and a right

After the Horse of the Year Show we started chasing points on the indoor World Cup circuit. St James was second in Berlin in the qualifier and ended up the year winning the Grand Prix and the World Cup Qualifier at Olympia, just like he had in 1983. We started off the new season by winning in Antwerp, but we drew a blank in Dortmund, and in Paris only picked up a minor place. By now Sarah was heavily pregnant and no longer able to travel to shows with me.

It was getting very difficult at the yard, the friction between me and Ted was getting worse and in the back of my mind, Sarah was about to give birth to my first child.

Daniel was born in Solihull Hospital on Tuesday, 9 April 1985. Sarah didn't want me to be at the birth so I was at home in Oak Cottage, waiting by the phone. As soon as she called me I went in and saw them both. It was a wonderful moment when I held my first child. The very next day we were due to leave for Gothenburg. I flew as the horses had gone on ahead in the horsebox.

John Whitaker, Malcolm Pyrah, David Broome and Liz were all riding there. On the first day our horses didn't go very well and then Ted arrived, not in the best of moods. He was giving out to Liz in the collecting ring, telling her she was bloody useless and couldn't ride and he was saying the same to me. I could see that he was now in a real temper and that I couldn't do or say anything right. My friends were all congratulating me on Daniel being born but there wasn't a word of congratulations from Ted.

Downstairs there was a Riders Club where you could get tea, coffee and snacks between classes. I went in there to keep my head down. Ted was talking to Eddie Macken but I didn't see Eddie at first. I walked in and sat down to have a drink. I didn't bother saying much to Ted because he wasn't really speaking to me. Eddie of course, didn't know what was going on so he jokingly said to Ted, 'You'll be getting a cot in the lorry now, will you?' To which Ted replied, 'That little bastard's not coming in my lorry.'

When I heard that I got up and walked out. I went back to the stables, absolutely seething and sat down thinking, 'Enough is enough.' I had had my fill of him. I knew I had to really think about my future. Ted had been shouting at Liz all day, he had been shouting at me all day, and now his spiteful remark was the straw that broke the camel's back.

I took my boots off and left the stables, it was between the afternoon and evening performances. I walked into the hotel foyer and Ted was sat on a sofa in reception, talking to Liz. As I walked across the foyer towards the lifts, Ted called, 'Where are you going, you useless fucker?'

I didn't say anything, I just ignored him and took the lift up to my room. After a while I went to see Malcolm Pyrah in his room where he was watching the racing on television; you can get BBC in Gothenburg. Malcolm could see that I was absolutely furious about something.

He asked, 'What's the matter with you?' I replied, 'If Ted says one more word to me I'm gonna knock his head off.'

'Now settle down, you don't want to be doing that here,' he advised but I was having none of it.

'I can't help myself, I've had enough. I can't take any more of this abuse.'

I watched a bit of racing with Malcolm and then went back to my room. Then the time came for me to go back to the stables for the evening performance. I took the lift back down to the foyer and I saw that Ted was still sitting with Liz on the sofa in reception. As I walked across he came out with another comment, which infuriated me. I was seeing red, my mind was a blank, I can't even remember what it was he said to me.

I walked over to him and said, 'Say that again.' And he did. So I lashed out and punched him twice, a left and a right. We ended up brawling on the floor in reception and for good measure I gave him a kick while we were down. At that point the hotel staff came and threw me out. After that it was a dismal show.

I walked down to the stables feeling much better, but I knew this was the end. I never saw Ted again during the show, he left and went home. Liz came down to the stables and I talked to her and explained what had happened, she fully understood how I felt.

I telephoned Sarah and told her about the fight but not the real reason why I hit Ted, that he had insulted my newborn son. I have never told anyone exactly the real reason until now. I believe people can abuse you as much as they like, but when they start abusing your family that can't be tolerated.

CHAPTER FOURTEEN
The End of the Road

I moved on to the World Cup Final in Berlin, worrying and thinking about the consequences of what I had done and the repercussions when I got home. But I had another week or ten days of the trip and I thought maybe it would all settle down. How wrong I was.

St James was in good form at Berlin. In the first leg we finished equal fifth with Malcolm Pyrah on Anglezarke. Michael won on Warren Point. When I telephoned the yard to report what had happened I had to talk to Liz, Ted wasn't speaking to me, as you can imagine.

I won the second leg, beating Malcolm who was second on Anglezarke, and Pierre Durand with Jappeloup, a horse I would meet again at the World Championships. St James and I were leading going into the last day. It really meant a lot for me to win this and redeem myself.

In the first round of the third leg, St James jumped clear but I still had Conrad Homfeld and Abdullah breathing down my neck. Abdullah was another horse I would meet at the World Championships the following year.

In the second round I only had to jump clear and I would win. The tension – with the Americans coming up behind me – was tremendous. If I won I would be the first European winner since Hugo Simon at the inaugural running of the World Cup.

Because I was leading I was last to go and Conrad had jumped a double clear. I was only three points in front of him. I had to jump clear. I couldn't make a mistake. I had the last but one fence down before the final double; there was a line of fences on a related distance of four strides and three strides, both of which were all a little bit long and St James was very, very unlucky, he just clipped the pole as he went up.

The first person I saw as I headed towards the competitors' stand was Frank Chapot, he was jumping out of his seat with his arms spread-eagled. Another American World Cup win! I ended up finishing second by one fault. Conrad finished on three faults and I finished on four.

I was gutted. Second is never good enough.

It was time to go home and face the music. The day of reckoning was here.

I turned up for work as normal at 7 a.m. to a not-so-good reception. Ted wouldn't speak to me at all, everything came via Liz.

New rules were being laid down. There was no way Ted wanted anything to do with me, so from now on I wasn't allowed in the house, not even for breakfast, and I wasn't allowed on the yard when Ted was there. I did everything with Liz. Ted never spoke to me for the next month, it was very difficult, and there seemed to be no way of smoothing things over.

I realised then that this was it, I would have to leave and set up on my own. The first thing I did was to call Terry Clemence who owned St James and tell him what had happened and that I would be going on my own. If I was going on my own I would need some horses with me. Terry, a good man, stood by me and said, 'Wherever you go, you can take my horse with you.' It was a great relief to know that I would have one of my best horses with me.

Then I rang Linda Jones who owned Apollo and she agreed the horse could come with me as well. I don't think they rang Ted and told him, they kept it to themselves.

Then I made a mistake. I suppose I should have stopped at two, but then I called Lady Inchcape and I didn't get the same response. I explained what had happened and asked if she would let me take Radius and Domino. She was less understanding. She sharply replied, 'Certainly not,' and implied that she could get a better jockey than me for her horses if I left Edgars.

By this time Ted had got wind of what I was up to, that I was ringing up the owners asking for their horses and it annoyed him, it rubbed more salt in the wound between us. So more new ground rules were laid down. I still don't know why to this day he didn't just kick me out and let me go. But he didn't, he just made me work on.

The latest set of new rules were that I would I arrive at the yard at 8 a.m. when Ted went in for breakfast and then leave again at 9 a.m. when he came back out. The only two horses I could ride were St James and Apollo. Our paths never crossed. I would still go to shows with Liz, as normal. At shows Ted would have nothing to do with me whatsoever. This went on all summer, but only working an hour a day gave me lots of free time to plan my future.

Dave Dick, a friend of both Ted's and mine, tried to intercede. I explained to him what had happened and he offered to talk to Ted and try and sort it out. Dicko went one day to speak to Ted, pointing out what a good winning team we had been, and couldn't things be sorted out between us. Ted agreed to let bygones be bygones. I went into the tractor shed where he was working and apologised to Ted while Dicko was there. We shook hands, I said I was sorry and we tried to get on as well as we could. But the rapprochement didn't last long, a couple of weeks went by and it reverted back. The damage had gone too deep and the rift never healed.

I started planning to set up on my own and Sarah and I went house hunting. We were looking for a place with stables and a bit of land but we didn't have much money. Our luck was in and we found an old farmhouse near Tapster Valley, in the heart of the Warwickshire countryside. It was in a quiet lane with good hacking for road work, although even then the M40 was planned which would eventually ruin the lovely view.

We sold Oak Cottage, took out a mortgage and bought Sandall House Farm. It was pretty run down, virtually derelict really; it had about ten acres with a stream running through the fields, a few old wooden stables along the side of a cracked concrete yard and a couple of pig sties. But it had loads of potential. The farmhouse wasn't fit to live in so Sarah, Daniel and I went and lived with my father and his wife Janette back at Odnaull End Farm.

In the meantime, I had said nothing back at the yard, but word soon got out.

One day in the lorry going to a show I told Liz that I would have to leave, that I couldn't go on like this any more. I offered to work to the end of the year and finish after Olympia. I asked her to tell Ted for me. She said she would. Liz was fine about it and completely understood.

We were a professional show jumping team though, so despite the problems, it was business as usual. The 1985 European Championships were held in August at Dinard and I was on the team with St James. John Whitaker had Hopscotch, Michael took Warren Point and Malcolm Pyrah rode Anglezarke.

We absolutely thrashed the opposition and won the Team Gold Medal by yards – our team finished on a total of 21.56 faults and the Swiss were second on 42.08. We had over five fences in hand.

We won the Team Gold Medal for three consecutive European Championships in equally good form. In 1987 we won in St Gallen (where I won Individual Bronze), with the same team except that John rode Milton, beating the French by 25.11 faults, over six fences in hand. In Rotterdam in 1989 we won by four fences, although on this occasion John was riding the great Milton; Michael was on Monsanta and I rode Apollo; Malcolm was replaced by Joe Turi riding Kruger. Compared with what's happening today in our sport, in those days the British were without doubt the best in Europe.

That show taught me that you should never give up. I was well down the field, twelfth or thirteenth, going into the last day for the Individual and didn't really think I had much of a chance, but Ronnie Massarella made me go. I went in to the ring half-heartedly. I wasn't trying very hard, all I really wanted to do was jump round and get out. I thought I had no chance at all. The third fence was a rustic oxer near the entrance and I let St James run into the fence and he had it down in front.

BUT, there were no clear rounds, so four faults was good enough and I moved up the placings quite a lot. In the last round I was more enthusiastic and we jumped the only clear, moving us up to fourth place. I could have ended up winning the Gold if only I hadn't been so stupid.

The fact that I had had a fist fight with Ted Edgar was the

scandal of all the shows and later on in August at the Hickstead Derby meeting I was interviewed by David Vine for the BBC. During the interview I announced that I was planning to leave the Edgars' stable at the end of the year.

Ted claimed that the television interview was the first he had heard of my plans to leave and that it was a shock to him. On 24 August 1985, Ted told Brian Giles of the Daily Mail, 'I'm not worried about him leaving my stable, but it would have been nicer if he had told me personally.'

'Absolute bollocks,' I thought.

Surely nobody in their right mind would think you could carry on a partnership where your paths never crossed? He must have been expecting it, even if Liz hadn't told him of our conversation.

On the same day I told Alan Smith of The Daily Telegraph, 'I'm twenty-eight and have decided it is time to make a life of my own. You wouldn't find a better trainer in the world than Ted Edgar and I think we have been a good team, but it couldn't last for ever.'

In the background, Sandall House Farm was taking shape and it was time to concentrate on getting new owners and sponsors. I knew I had St James and Apollo but I needed more horses. Sarah was pleased with developments, she didn't like Ted any more than he liked her.

While at Hickstead I had been talking to a good friend of mine, David Bowen, and he had suggested that I should talk to Tony Elliott, who was David's main owner. Tony agreed to set me up with a lorry and a string of horses which was great news for me and Sarah. It was a private deal, not corporate sponsorship, which made it especially generous of him.

Shortly afterwards I was approached by Raffles Cigarettes who were already sponsoring Helena Dickinson, who is now married to Peter Weinberg the German rider. They asked if I would I be interested in any sponsorship – I thought, 'YES!'

I was thinking that about £50,000 annually would be nice, back in 1985 that was a lot of money. A week or two later I bumped into Paddy McMahon and his wife Tricia at a local show and she asked me if I had found a sponsor yet, so I told her about the Raffles deal. Tricia had done a very good job for Paddy with Toyota and she offered to get me double the figure I was thinking of but she asked for ten per cent commission. I told her to go ahead and see what she could do.

Sure enough, Tricia came up with the goods and Raffles sponsored me to the tune of £100,000 annually for three years. That really helped to put me on my feet and build Sandall House Farm. What I didn't realise at the time, was that I also had a contract with Tricia McMahon as my agent which later on cost me thousands of pounds to get out of. When the Raffles sponsorship ended, Tricia was unable to come up with a new sponsor but in the meantime I had found Burmah Castrol for myself. Tricia, as my agent, insisted that I could not have them as a sponsor because I was contracted to her, even though she had not found me a new sponsor. In the end, I had to pay up!

Tricia subsequently went to jail a few years later for a totally unrelated incident.

$100,000

Like I say, it was business as usual, and in September I flew to Calgary with St James and Apollo.

It was a show of real ups and downs. St James won the big class the first day and I fell off Apollo on the second day. It had rained a lot and although the ground wasn't bad, it was muddy. St James was a mud lover but Apollo didn't really like it.

At Spruce Meadows, the big money classes are at the weekend, and the day after I fell off Apollo he won a class, despite the ground.

In the Nations Cup on the Saturday, Ronnie Massarella wanted me to ride St James but I wanted to ride Apollo for the team and keep St James for the Grand Prix on the Sunday with a vast first prize of £38,000.

Ronnie and I had quite a squabble about this but in the end I got my own way. Ronnie was not at all happy and he threatened that if Apollo didn't go well in the Nations Cup he would make sure I went up in front of the hierarchy (the selectors) when I got home. He told me, 'Your neck's on the line.'

Apollo jumped two clear rounds in the Nations Cup on the Saturday, which got me off the hook. Then on the Sunday, Apollo came out and won the Speed Derby and St James jumped the only two clear rounds in the Du Maurier Grand Prix and won the £38,000.

As I wasn't allowed in the house, back at Edgars on the Monday morning I put a cheque for about $100,000 through the letterbox of Ted's back door. More than we had ever won before, but he still wasn't having anything to do with me.

As I let go of the cheque and it fell on the mat, I remember thinking what a pity it wasn't next year when I would be on my own. In hindsight, I would have been better leaving a year early as St James was really at his peak, 1985 was his best year.

CHAPTER FIFTEEN

Going Alone

I lived the next couple of months in a complete haze and have very little recollection of the detail. I was worrying about the future, going it alone with a wife and child to support, the whole thing. It was a big step into the unknown.

Finally, Ted and I parted and I moved my family into Sandall House Farm in November, I think. We had a few stables for the horses and the house was now fit for human habitation.

David Bowen had been to Paul Schockemöhle's PSI sale in November and bought two more good young horses for me to ride – Grand Slam and Duell – as well as a horse called Feiner Kerl that he bought in Spain. So I had three horses to ride for Tony Elliot as well as Apollo and St James who had settled down in their new home. Tony very generously provided me with a horsebox so I could get them to Olympia where the three-year Raffles sponsorship was announced. Things were looking up.

Sally Mapleson, a team-mate from Junior days, was at Olympia and she told me she was giving up competing and wanted to send me her two best horses, Airbourne and Rhapsody. Sure to her word, a few weeks later on 11 January they arrived and she even sent her own groom, Mark Beever, to help me out. Sally's words were, 'I'll send Mark with the horses to help for a while until you find somebody. But he won't put up with you, he'll never work for somebody like you, you are too bossy.'

Those were famous last words; sixteen years later Mark Beever is still working for me – apart from a couple of weeks last year when he sacked himself and went AWOL!

Throughout those formative years, Mark travelled to all the

NICK SKELTON ONLY FALLS AND HORSES

international shows with me and made a major contribution to my success. Utterly professional and competent with a thorough understanding of horses, I would not like to have had to manage without him. Mark is known all over the world as being one of the best grooms in show jumping. One of the grooms from Edgars, Susie, had left when I did and she was also working for me. So Mark and Susie did the horses between them.

Daniel was now five months old and Sarah was riding again. She had two horses that belonged to Mike and Sue Phillips, good friends of ours, and Mike was a great help to us when we were renovating the house. Mike worked for Sankeys and was able to give us a really good deal on all the radiators, bathroom and kitchen equipment. We always appreciated that help, as we couldn't have managed with out it. Thanks Mike!

Not long after Mark arrived with Sally's horses, I left for New Zealand with Michael Mac and Tony Newbury where we had been invited to compete on borrowed horses.

Tony was married to commentator David Coleman's daughter Ann, and her brother Dean kept a bar and restaurant in Auckland. So, our first task upon arrival was to find Dean. He turned out to be great fun, a very talented entertainer. He loved having fun and hadn't seen Tony for years, so he was determined we would have a good time.

We rounded up a party of riders including Katie Monahan, Lynne Little, Mark Laskin and Trevor Graham, an Irish dealer who now lives in America. Dean wisely put us at a table at the back of the restaurant next to a stairwell.

He then introduced us to a drink called a B52 Bomber. I think it was a mix of Kahlua, Baileys, Grenadine and Drambuie. The two American girls were a bit restrained but we lads were getting well stuck into these B52 Bombers, drinking like they were going out of fashion.

It ended up that every time we drank one down, we threw the glasses over our shoulders where they hit the wall and fell shattered down the stairwell. The two girls didn't think much of our behaviour. Dean thought it was great fun, he didn't mind at all and just kept sending fresh glasses of B52s. In the end the girls started

CHIO

Nr. 1   17-08-'90

Het CHIO Journaal is een
uitgave van de
Stichting CHIO Rotterdam,
in samenwerking met BCM/
Equestrian Communications.

Medewerkers:
Ton Corbeau
Fernande van Dunné
Pien Engelsman
Bert Huisman
Henk Rottinghuis
Fotograaf: Arnd Bronkhorst
Druk: Tromp Drukkerij B.V.
Rotterdam

43 JAAR ROTTERDAM '90

Te water ...

Het ging zo goed met de
Engelse springruiter Nick
Skelton. Het concours was
nog maar net begonnen of hij
won al een wedstrijd en werd
een keer tweede. Maar toen
was er op donderdagmiddag
de hindernis met die sloot.
„Je bekijkt het maar", moet
zijn paard hebben gedacht
toen hij voor de derde maal
voor de waterpartij werd ge-
zet. Alan Paul Major Wager
stopte wederom en met zo-
veel overtuiging dat zijn rui-
ter met een flinke plons in het
water verdween.

Top: Going, going
Above: Gone! Major Wager depositing
me in the water jump at Rotterdam
Right: Opening ceremony at Seoul 1988.
l-r I am third from left, Joe Turi is fifth from
left, Malcolm Pyrah is sixth from left and
Ronnie Massarella is seventh from left

Above: Major Wager jumping at his first show at Church Farm. He was the most careful horse ever had

Below: Grand Slam in Aachen. His ears were always forward - you can tell by the look on his face what a genuine horse he was

Right: Limited Edition winning the King George V Gold Cup at Hickstead. Lord King presenting the trophy. Guy Goosen (right) was second
Below: Warren Clarke and I with Benjamin and Dollar Girl exercising in the sea at La Baule
Bottom: Wassup!!! With Adrian Maguire having a Bud on holiday in Bermuda

Above: Dollar Girl relaxing in her whirlpool and listening in on my conversation with Cilla. She was such an intelligent horse, look at the expression on her face
Below: Daniel, Harry and me taking time out at Hickstead

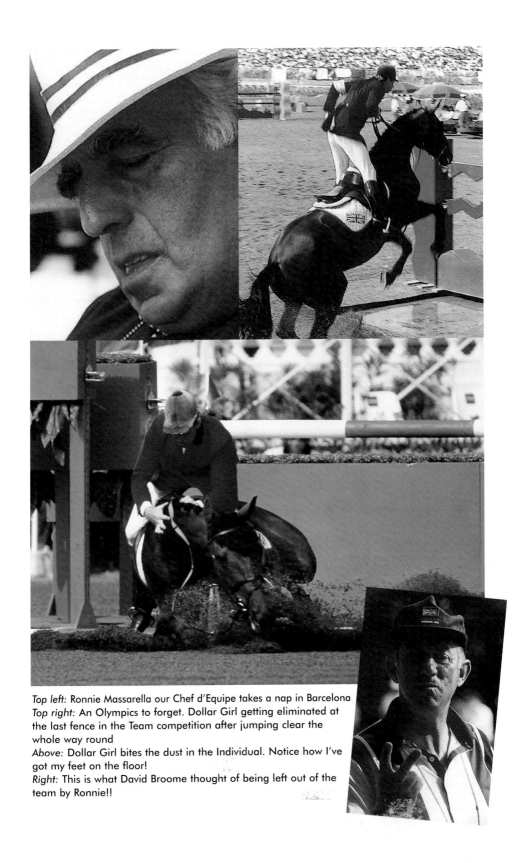

Top left: Ronnie Massarella our Chef d'Equipe takes a nap in Barcelona
Top right: An Olympics to forget. Dollar Girl getting eliminated at
the last fence in the Team competition after jumping clear the
whole way round
Above: Dollar Girl bites the dust in the Individual. Notice how I've
got my feet on the floor!
Right: This is what David Broome thought of being left out of the
team by Ronnie!!

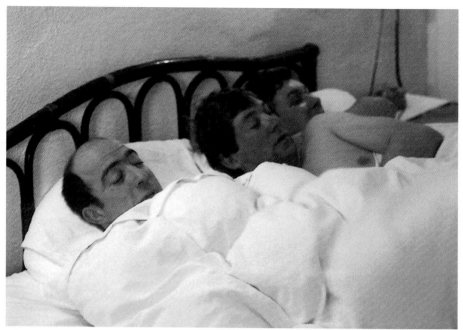

Above: After a heavy night in the bar at Kossen. Michael Whitaker, myself and Geoff Billington being woken up by Chris Goosen the photographer
Below: Later the same day - competing on the snow riding Shakespeare for Steven Hadley

Above: My dad and I watching my first trained runner, Jolly Roger, at Barbury Castle Point to Point
Below: Adrian Maguire and Certainly Strong coming in at Haydock Park
This was Adrian's 500th win and David Nicholson's 1000th

Above: At Birmingham winning my sponsors class, Alan Paul Hairdressing, with Fiorella. Mike Rowland on the left and the late Alan Moss presenting me with the trophy
Below: Top Gun winning the Grand Prix in Dortmund. It was a sad day when I lost this horse

to join in and they were slinging their empty glasses down the stairwell, too. Whenever I see Katie nowadays I always remind her about the B52s.

The next night Dean took us to a nightclub; well, Michael Mac was like a kid in a sweet shop. The place was full of stunningly beautiful women. But Dean, who didn't sing to the same hymn sheet as us, had told Tony and me that this was a transvestites' club. The 'women' were so glamorous, dressed up like dogs dinners. Mackie was well away and we decided not to tell him and see what happened.

Tony and I went to the bar and ordered a drink; Mackie was on the edge of the dance floor with his mouth open, ogling all these sexy 'girls'. We took our drinks and wandered back over. Mackie was being chatted up; he thought he had pulled. We tapped him on the shoulder and whispered, 'Do you realise, that's not a girl?' He was so on for pulling this bird, he just couldn't believe it. He was shell-shocked. It completely took the wind out of his sails, so we drank up and beat a retreat.

On the way home, we stopped off for a short break in Honolulu and stayed at the Royal Hawaiian Hotel. They did great breakfasts there, I highly recommend them.

We can't have behaved too badly because we were all invited back to New Zealand the next year. This time we took David Bowen with us. We flew from Gatwick but the flight was two or three hours late departing. Upon arrival in Houston we discovered that the connecting flight had left without us so we had to stay overnight. This meant passing through Immigration control but David didn't have a visa for entry into the US. So we went off to a hotel for the night and David was taken away, along with a few other passengers, to be held overnight under a sort of house arrest in secure accommodation!

Next morning, we arrived at the airport to catch the plane to Los Angeles but couldn't find David Bowen. We asked round and Immigration had put him on the very first available flight out to LA. I can understand why, anyone who knows David would! The authorities would have been desperate to get rid of him.

The connecting flight from LA. to Honolulu was delayed as

well, so while we waited we looked around for David. Finally, we came across him, asleep on a bench. From Honolulu we flew on to Auckland where we arrived absolutely shattered. It had taken us days to get there.

World Championships

1986 was a World Championship year and they were to be held in Aachen. I took both my best horses but contested the World Championships with Apollo who had started the year well, winning classes in Jerez, Madrid and Barcelona.

I was on the team with Malcolm and Anglezarke, John and Hopscotch and Michael with Warren Point. We had a show the week before in Wolfsburg and stopped over and did a bit of team training. We got wind of it that at Aachen the next week, the German course builders were planning to put a full-size water jump in the middle of the combination. This had never been tried before. Anyway, we practised this novelty fence in Wolfsburg and sure enough, on the first day at Aachen, the combination was a vertical, two strides to a full-size water jump and then two strides to an oxer going out.

The first day was a bit of a disaster. Hopscotch was eliminated and never went again during the show. Warren Point wasn't up to his usual form but Michael did a fantastic job on him to get round as best he could. We ended up being beaten by the Americans who took the Gold Medal – Michael Matz with Chef, Conrad Homfeld and Abdullah, Katie Monohan on Amadia, and Katherine Burdsall riding The Natural. They beat us by only one fault I seem to recall, we won the Silver Medal.

Going into the last day before the Final, Anglezarke and Malcolm were within striking distance but Pierre Durand's Jappeloup and Conrad with Abdullah were well ahead.

However, I had learned my lesson about never giving up I and stayed optimistic. In the end Malcolm's bad luck was my good luck. Just before the last round Anglezarke tipped up in the collecting ring and couldn't go on. In the last round I jumped into fourth, basically taking Malcolm's place. Pierre, Conrad and I were joined by the little-known, young Canadian rider Gail Greenhough and her horse Mr T.

Now I was in the final four. The Individual World Championship is a unique competition. The top four riders go through to a final in which they jump a round on each of the four horses. The rider with the least number of faults from all four horses is proclaimed World Champion. Unlike the Olympic Games or European Championships, the aim is to find the best rider, not the best horse-and-rider combination. However, that view is not necessarily shared by the riders! When interviewed at the time, Conrad Homfeld commented that the competition was like a lottery and the result was in the lap of the gods.

The draw plays a big part in the competition as clear rounds depend very much on which rider you follow on each horse. If a horse has a bad time with a rider and you then have to ride the same horse directly afterwards, then the horse is upset and it may not jump so well for you. So the draw is important.

Saturday was a day off and all the riders were being interviewed on television, and the question being asked was which horse they feared riding the most. Everyone, including me, said, 'Apollo!' In fact, Pierre Durand looked quite ill at the prospect of riding my horse.

On the Sunday morning Robert Smith was there to support me and we walked the course together. Riders were allowed to take somebody into the arena to help them because the only chance you have to warm up on each different horse is over two fences in the main ring, right there in front of the audience.

We each jumped a round on our own horses; Pierre had two down on Jappeloup but Gail, Conrad and I were all clear. I felt a sense of relief, I had jumped clear on Apollo, the horse I felt sure was the most difficult to ride. Or so I thought.

The atmosphere was great, there were about 60,000 people there in the stadium.

I jumped clear on Abdullah and then clear again on Jappeloup who gave me the most unbelievable feeling I have ever had on a horse. The more you held him, the more you squeezed him, the higher he jumped. But Gail Greenhough was also going well, jumping clear on both of them. I had jumped three clear rounds and so had Gail. Now I had to ride Gail's Mr T and she had to ride Apollo.

I remember getting on Mr T after Pierre had ridden him; the minute I hit the saddle the horse was like a time bomb waiting to explode. He was really fired up. The moment I touched the reins and tried to hold him he overreacted. He was very, very delicate to ride. Then I made a serious error of judgment. I thought I'd try and ride him like Gail rode him, just sit very quiet, don't do much, not too much hand, not a lot of leg.

Mr T was getting fairly strong and buzzy underneath me and going down to the combination I didn't know whether to pull, push, or what, so I just sat very still. No hand, no leg, nothing. Two strides away he broke into a trot so I gave him a big kick. That wasn't a good idea. He stopped, put his head on the fence and fell into it. Goodbye World Champion! That was definitely one of the biggest disappointments of my life. I should have got on him and ridden him properly, kept him between hand and leg, like you should. I rode him like a complete fairy and threw the World Championships away.

Mind you, I would have had to have jumped clear on him because Gail jumped clear on every horse, including Apollo. Then we would have jumped off against each other, on our own horses, and who knows what would have happened.

I was watching Gail ride Apollo and I turned to Robert and said, 'Don't worry, Apollo'll take care of her in a minute,' but he didn't. She rode him very well and Apollo seemed to like the novelty of a lightweight girl on his back. The whole competition was screened on Channel 4 as part of The Horse in Sport and thankfully they edited my comment, so on television I only said, 'Apollo'll take of her,' a double entendre!

Gail had gone into that final thinking she would end up fourth, she went in there just to enjoy herself. She admits that. She had no pressure on her at all and she ended up doing a brilliant job. I ended up with ten faults and finished third. Conrad was second with Abdullah and Gail won. The system works well for some, but not for others. I felt sorry for Pierre because he and Jappeloup were such a brilliant horse-and-rider combination and together they went on to win the Individual Gold Medal at the Seoul Olympics and the European Championships.

Conrad Homfeld didn't ride very much afterwards. I honestly think it finished him off. I don't know whether he couldn't get over not winning, or maybe it was being beaten by Gail, but he didn't ride a lot after that. In a television interview prior to the competition he had said, 'It's a lottery, it's in the lap of the gods now.' Clearly he hadn't been praying.

CHAPTER SIXTEEN
Irish Hospitality

By 1986 St James was starting to feel his age; like I said, 1985 was his best year. He was sixteen years old and had worked hard for me but he was getting towards the end of his career. I really was considering calling time on him. I like to retire my horses before the end, while they are still enjoying the job. He was getting old and a bit arthritic; keeping him sound was starting to become a problem so I didn't do so many shows with him.

Apollo was now taking over the top slot in the yard. From the World Championships in Aachen we had moved on to Dublin where Apollo won the Puissance, jumping 7ft 3in and we were also on the winning Nations Cup team.

Dublin is always a fantastic show and invariably, year after year, something momentous always happens, but not usually in the show jumping ring!

I remember another time, when Ireland won the Nations Cup. Con Power – Captain Con – was the hero of the team. I was there with Mick Saywell who was riding Chainbridge.

After Ireland won the Nations Cup, Mick Saywell and myself ended up having a few drinks with him in the bar. We still had our boots and breeches on and were getting a bit on the rowdy side. After the Nations Cup we always had to go to the British Embassy to meet the Ambassador and we would always have a few drinks there and a bit of a party. We were drinking in the bar and Ronnie said, 'Now don't be late lads, hurry up, be back in the bus in ten minutes to go to the embassy.'

Mick told his wife Vicky to go back to the hotel and get changed and he would take her out for dinner later when he returned from the embassy. At which, off Vicky trotted. Still in our boots and breeches, we climbed into the mini bus along with the rest of the team. At the embassy we had a few more drinks and Mick and I started to get even rowdier than we had been in the bar at the show.

When we left the embassy to go back to the hotel, Ronnie, for some reason, put his suit jacket in the mini bus. He was following us in a car driven by Orson Welles' daughter, who he knew quite well. The mini bus was full, he had no choice. But we had Ronnie's jacket in the bus.

We were driving on down through Dublin, Ronnie following us with the young lady, when Mick and I decided it would be a good idea to open the back door and throw Ronnie's jacket out in the road. As you do. So we opened the door and flung it out, to a great round of applause from the other lads on the bus. We all watched with glee as Ronnie's car drove straight over it. The young lady had to pull up and stop so Ronnie could retrieve his jacket from the middle of the road. 'We're for it now, Mick,' I said.

But it was worse than we thought; somebody had given Ronnie a pot of strawberry jam and he had put it in his jacket pocket!

Anyway, we didn't see any more of Ronnie that evening and when we got back to the showground we met up with Con Power again. Con being a Captain, there was a party on in the army barracks because the Irish team had won the Nations Cup, so off we went to the barracks. Con was absolutely flying by now, standing up with his cap on and his full army dress, head out of the sun roof, saluting all the passersby as we drove through the centre of Dublin.

When we arrived at the barracks we had a few more, but just around midnight, I turned to Mick, 'Oi, what about Vicky? Do you think she'll have got dressed for dinner by now?'

'Oh shit,' he replied, 'I forgot all about her.'

Well, the damage was already done, it was too late for dinner, so Mick decided we may as well carry on. Chainbridge had put a foot in the water in the Nations Cup earlier that day, and with it being the Grand Prix the next day we figured the horse was going to go in again. So after quite a few drinks, we thought we better go back and train him over the water, in the main ring, (which isn't allowed), like back at the Cock O' The North.

We were still in our breeches and boots so this seemed like a sensible idea at the time and we got a lift back to the stables. But it was starting to get light, and when we got back to the showground it was too late, everyone was getting up; there was no way we could get the horse out, never mind use the main ring. There were far too many people about. We left the showground and wandered down Simmons Court Road looking for a taxi, at six o'clock in the morning. Irish taxi drivers expect to find a fare at that time of the morning, so we had no problem finding one.

Then we suddenly remembered Vicky again. Thank God I wasn't sharing a room with Mick, because he had to face up to her when he got back in.

Apparently, as Mick tells the story, he said to her, 'Now listen here Vicky, they're all expecting you to be in a real foul mood with me this morning, but just play it along that there's nothing wrong at all.' Vicky came down in the morning and played the part to the hilt. She was perfectly cheerful. We were all envious that she was so tolerant.

However, when Mick and I arrived at the show later in the day, Ronnie said, 'I wanna see you two,' and sure enough we got a right bollocking.

'I'm sick of your bad language,' he told us. 'And your behaviour. Any more of it and you're gonna be in front of the stewards.' He gave us a proper telling off. I think it was the shattered strawberry jam jar that annoyed him so much, not our high spirits.

Good old Ronnie. I'll tell you one thing about Ronnie Massarella, over all the years I was in his teams, he always looked after us boys as best he could. He never ever wanted us to get into trouble, he always tried to protect us.

The Killing Fields

Sarah and I had been living at Sandall House Farm for nearly a year now, and the place was really taking shape. The pig sties were converted into four loose boxes attached to the side of the house; a block of nine wooden stables were built along the edge of the concrete yard; and an outhouse on the other side of the house was converted into a stable. We were shoving horses in all over the place.

The indoor school, not very big but a good strong building, had a floor of dirt and shavings. Up until I sold the farm just a few years ago, the indoor school still had dirt and shavings on the floor. It was perfectly adequate throughout all those years, I never felt the need for one of those expensive surfaces.

While I was in Aachen in 1986, I had noticed a lad constantly following me around. Whenever I went to the arena he followed me, whenever I warmed up he followed me, taking pictures the whole time and in the end I was getting a bit worried. He was starting to get on my nerves, it was like being stalked. For the whole week he watched every move I made.

Then one day towards the end of the year, I got a telephone call from a Spanish lad. In broken English he told me, 'I was the person following you around at Aachen. Would it be possible for me to come to England to learn to ride with you and train with you?' His name was Alfredo Fernandez Duran and he was twenty-two years old.

He just wanted to come and help and I thought yes, that's just the sort of person I need. I remembered him as a strong-looking lad, and we were starting to do a lot of farm work, fencing, railing, ditching. It was January and I told him to bring plenty of warm clothes, 'It's not like living in Madrid here, it's pretty bleak,' I told him.

Alfredo turned up and the whole time he stayed I had him carrying posts and rails all over the fields we were fencing. He had to carry them, I didn't have a tractor and trailer, and so he used to carry them on his shoulders. Back and forth to the yard, fetching more rails and posts. Alfredo named my farm 'The Killing Fields'!

He became a good friend to me and went on to ride at the Seoul Olympics with Kaoua, a horse I helped him buy. He rides very much in my style although he only got to ride two horses during his stay. It seems he learned a lot from me even though he hardly ever rode!

St James is lost forever

St James really wasn't up to his best any more by 1987 and I decided to tell Terry Clemence that I thought the horse should be retired. He'd been a good servant and deserved a good rest and retirement.

Terry didn't think along the same lines and was convinced the horse still had something left in him so he wanted me to take the horse down to Geoffrey Brain at Bourton on the Water and get a complete veterinary report. Clearly, Terry didn't believe what I was telling him.

That is one of the problems you run up against with owners who are not horse people; a lot of them think their animals are just money-making machines.

I told Geoffrey Brain the situation, that I thought St James had had enough, and he gave a full veterinary report that in his opinion the horse should be retired as well. Despite the report from Geoffrey Brain, Terry Clemence sent the horse back to the Edgars for Marie, Ted and Liz's daughter, to ride but it was all to no avail and St James was retired later in 1987 along with Maybe at Terry's home, The Woodhouse, in Epping.

The house was eventually sold to Rod Stewart and Maybe was left there because Norma, who used to groom St James for me, stayed on at The Woodhouse when Rod bought it and to my knowledge, she is still there now.

St James moved home with the Clemence's to their new house in Weybridge where Sarah Jane rang me one day to say that St James had injured a tendon out in the field. They tried to operate and give him a carbon fibre implant so he could continue his retirement, but I was told a while later that he had died.

J Nick

David Bowen owned a horse called J Nick, which he had been riding himself but he decided to send it to me and let me try it. I rode the horse and it went well for me, whereupon David sold it to Tony Elliot for me to ride.

J Nick was supposed to be by a horse called Wily Trout, an Irish thoroughbred, not Chris Bartle's dressage horse! Sure enough, he was a wily character.

He arrived at the yard in the winter and was very hairy but it wasn't long before Mark Beever discovered you couldn't clip his legs. We even tried putting him on the lorry and jamming him between two partitions so Mark could clip his legs, but J Nick was having none of it. He had a lot of feather in his heels but he hated having them clipped. He couldn't bear having his legs touched, even putting tendon boots or bandages on him was a nightmare.

He was a strong-minded, strong-willed character and he was physically strong as well. He was a very talented horse and had a great jumping technique; but he was quite hot to ride, his character let him down, he wasn't easy. Although as time went on, with careful handling, he got a lot better.

Like If Ever, J Nick didn't actually win many classes but the classes he did win were good ones.

The week before Hickstead Derby we were at a show in Gijón on the north coast of Spain. I had taken J Nick along with Airbourne who was well on his way to becoming a top-class horse; I was riding him in the Nations Cup team along with Janet Hunter and Lisnamarrow, Malcolm with Anglezarke and John on Hopscotch. Janet, Malcolm and I all jumped clear and, as fourth team member, John didn't need to go because the score was zero. We all jumped clear in the next round as well, so again, John didn't have to go in to the ring. At the prize giving John collected £2,000 and a Brietling watch and he hadn't even got out of the stands!

But J Nick was less obliging and was proving a bit difficult. I rode him in a thick loose ring snaffle and he was pulling me around.

Gijón finished on the Monday and it was a good three days' drive to Hickstead for the Derby meeting. John Whitaker and I were still sharing a lorry to travel to shows, and Clare Whitaker was driving. I was really annoyed with J Nick because he had not gone well and I asked Clare to 'Get that horse over to Hickstead, quick as you can.' I think she drove day and night to get there in time, arriving at Hickstead in the early hours of Friday morning, the day of the Derby Trial.

I virtually pulled him straight off the lorry and jumped him in the Derby Trial. He came out full of energy, bucking and kicking, not at all like a horse who had travelled for three days. And he still mauled me all round the Derby Trial. I think he had one fence down.

On the Saturday he was still running away with me so I lunged him for an hour or so. I figured I had to wear him out or I'd never be able to hold him going round the Derby. I gave up with the loose ring snaffle and put a twisted wire bit in his mouth. I hadn't tried him in a different bit before. I still couldn't hold one side of him; the Derby Bank felt like a speed bump in the road, he went up and down it so quick I barely noticed it. But he jumped the only clear round and won.

Horror

By now, Tony Elliot was accumulating a lot of horses in my yard, all of them promising, talented animals including Serenade, bought from the American rider Leslie Burr. The lorry he had loaned to me was painted in Raffles colours and the whole set-up had a very professional air to it. It was the year of the Seoul Olympics and life was looking up.

I've said it before about ups and downs, but I'll say it again. There's no substitute for horses when it comes to the fact that an up is always followed by a down.

At a show in Bethune, a little French village, I was warming up J Nick to go in the ring. I got off to adjust my saddle and thought, 'I'll just have one more vertical.' J Nick was a very active jumper, when he came to take off at a fence he really bounded off the floor. We went down to a vertical and took off. I heard this strange 'squelch' noise. He landed on three legs and stopped dead, throwing his left foreleg around.

I leapt off to find blood everywhere. For a horse that you couldn't do anything to, he suddenly became a very sober, obliging animal. I looked down and saw that he had over-reached so badly that he had pulled off his hoof. It was held on by three inches around the front of the coronet band, the pedal bone was exposed, the hoof was off. It was horrific.

Bethune was a little country show out in the middle of nowhere and there was no show vet. Andrew Saywell was grooming for me and coped with the trauma really well. Everyone was running round looking for a vet. J Nick was bleeding profusely and the nearest Equine Clinic to take him to was in Belgium. In the lorry I just happened to have some plaster of Paris, so we filled him with painkillers, pushed the hoof back on as best we could and made a plaster cast to contain the injured foot.

We loaded the horse on to the lorry and drove him to the Clinic, having telephoned Dr Peter Cronau, a leading German veterinary surgeon. He was in the south of Germany but hurriedly drove up through the night to meet us at the clinic. J Nick was put on the operating table but after investigation Dr Cronau said there was no way he could repair the foot. All the arteries were broken. It was inoperable and they put him down while under the anaesthetic.

These things often go in threes and I wondered what the next serious incident would be.

Plankety plank

After that awful experience, things improved. For the second consecutive year I won the Derby.

Apollo took to the Derby course like a duck to water. He loved it. It suited his cross-country approach to life. I guess that is why he made such a good hunter when he retired.

Apollo was always forward-going and strong, he gave me a good ride round the Derby. He was great for the big occasion and Apollo knew the Derby was a big occasion. He went on to win it the following year in 1989, giving me three consecutive Derby wins, and he was second three times; he came to know the course quite well. Over the Derby Bank he was foot perfect, it didn't feel like a speed bump.

Although he wasn't always foot perfect. At New York one year the course builder had included some very light, fragile, airy, little planks. Apollo had had them down two days running and I felt sure that if they were used in the Grand Prix course he would kick them out again. I figured that the best way of guaranteeing he wouldn't knock the planks down was to eliminate them.

So that night, dead sober, before I'd had a drink, I hung around until everybody had gone and then I went and found the planks which were kept on a trailer in the collecting ring. I took all three and hid them on top of a pile of pallets stacked in the corner of the stable complex. That's that, I thought, they won't be in the Grand Prix tomorrow.

The next day when I went to walk the course, I couldn't believe my eyes. I must have missed one. Right there, going into the combination, was a single plank at about 1.5m with a brush fence underneath it. I was drawn near the end of the class and early on I thought my luck had changed. An American rider went in, had a stop at the plank; the horse put his head on it and smashed it clean in half. There was a five-minute delay while the course builders went looking for the planks again and when they still couldn't find them, they came back with a piece of wood, a hammer and some nails and proceeded to repair the broken plank.

The class continued and about twenty minutes went by before a member of the arena party eventually found the hidden planks and came running in to replace the broken one. As it happened, Apollo jumped the single plank fine, the brush underneath set him off it a bit.

CHAPTER SEVENTEEN
Seoul Olympics

Leaving Edgars had been the right decision. I was making it on my own and it was very satisfying. Sally Mapleson's Airbourne and Tony Elliot's Grand Slam were developing into good horses, my string were going well.

Apollo was definitely my top horse though, winning the 1987 Aachen Grand Prix and he was on the Gold Medal winning team at the European Championships that same year. We finished third in the Individual, behind John Whitaker on Milton and Pierre Durand who won the Gold on Jappeloup. This put Apollo right up there with Milton and Jappeloup, undoubtedly two of the best horses in the world.

The rules for Olympic qualification had changed and I was now the holder of a competitor's licence. This meant that despite being a sponsored rider, I was not considered 'professional' and was eligible for Olympic competition. 1988 being an Olympic year, I focused on the Seoul Olympics that were being held in September to take advantage of the cooler, less humid weather.

I was having a successful season, Apollo won Aachen for the second successive year and he also won the Dublin Grand Prix. He was on form, and I was hopeful of an Olympic medal. Seoul would be the furthest I had ever travelled with a horse and – having joined in the boycott at Moscow – it would be my first full-blown Olympics.

The team was named: David Broome with Countryman; Joe Turi with Kruger and Vital; Malcolm Pyrah with Anglezarke; and me with Apollo. Michael Whitaker was travelling reserve with Amanda. We were a strong team, but not as strong as we should have been. We had had to leave behind our best horse – Milton.

Milton didn't go to Seoul because his owners, Mr and Mrs Bradley, said they feared for the health of their horse. They used the excuse that the conditions would be dirty, hot and humid; there was a war on in Korea, it couldn't be a very nice place.

But in truth, I think it was a bit of a tit for tat against the BSJA, who several years before had dropped Caroline from a previous Olympic team. It seemed as if they were getting their own back. It was a pity for John, though, because Milton was at his very, very best and that was his chance of winning Olympic Gold.

But what incredible entertainment the Olympics were. It was a laugh from start to finish. It was a good trip. We stayed in the Athletes Village where Broomie was our fall guy, we took the piss out of him mercilessly. Graham Fletcher came along as our trainer, adding to the mayhem.

It all started at the airport. There we all were, in our Olympic tracksuits; everyone looked exactly the same. The plane was full of Olympic athletes, and every single one of us had the same Olympic suitcase. Trying to find your own suitcase at Seoul airport was shaping up to be a complete farce. There would be hundreds of red suitcases, all going round together on the carousel.

David Broome walked in wearing his tracksuit and baseball cap. He didn't look very athletic so I called over to him, 'Shot putters, that way!' Poor Broomie. We gave him a barrage of abuse on that trip. One night he even tried to throttle me out on the balcony of our apartment in the Village. You really have to be able to get on well with people there, sharing accommodation for three weeks.

Our apartment had four bedrooms and two bathrooms with a lounge and kitchen area. The bedrooms were pretty basic. The sheets and pillow cases appeared to be made of Jeye cloth, there was lino on the floor and the wardrobe looked like a metal gun case. This was no five-star hotel!

I roomed with Michael, Malcolm shared with Joe Turi, David bunked down with Fletch, and Ronnie was honoured with a room to himself. Nobody wanted to share with Ronnie anyway because he can snore for England. Ronnie always won the Gold Medal for snoring in our camp, he was undisputed champion.

With there being only two bathrooms, there were four of us in one and three in the other. Maids would come in and clean twice a week, but it wasn't often enough. Ronnie and David are both a bit precious so they shared a bathroom and only allowed Fletch in under protest. They were very possessive about their bathroom.

David hated getting out of bed and having to put his feet on the cold lino. He also hated getting out of the bath and putting his feet on the cold floor. So the first thing he did was to go and buy a bath mat and a bit of carpet so he could get out of bed in comfort.

Michael and I used to go and nick his bath mat in the night and put it in our bathroom and put his bit of carpet between our beds. And we four all used to go and use his toilet before he got up! This kept our bathroom smelling sweet which we thought was a bonus.

There was a communal launderette in the building of the apartments, where we had to do our own washing. We could tell that Fletch wasn't domesticated because he didn't know you had to put washing powder in an automatic washing machine. He thought an automatic washing machine was completely automatic and didn't need powder.

And we turned heads one day when we walked into the Village through the airport-type security scanners; Michael was carrying 200 Silk Cut and Fletch was toting a case of Carlsberg under each arm. How about that for Olympic athletes?

You see some funny sights at the Olympics. Every morning at breakfast you could get any sort of food you wanted, from anywhere in the world. It must be a catering nightmare. But my most vivid memory is of a Mongolian female basketball player. She must have been 6ft 7in with size 15 feet. She didn't bother with a plate she just put the food straight on to the tray, as much as she could stack on. Even Broomie couldn't eat as much as did.

The Athletes Village was very close to the Olympic Stadium and the horses were stabled about half an hour away. You couldn't have wished for a better, cleaner, more efficiently operated equestrian complex in the world than at Seoul. Of all the Olympics I have been to it has been the best.

Our wives were staying at a doss house that called itself a hotel, out near the equestrian complex. We all used to go out together in the evening for meals in restaurants and then we lads would go back to the Athletes Village. Ronnie liked to keep the Olympic team atmosphere. He was absolutely right, and it was an experience I wouldn't have missed for the world.

Another good thing about Seoul was the market in the city, called Ei-Tai-Wan. That's where they used to sell all the hookey fake designer gear. Watches, T-shirts, suitcases, shoes, handbags, Louis Vuitton, Gucci, you name it, they had it. One day David bought himself a Rolex watch for about $20 and later that night we were out for dinner with Lord Harris, who owned Countryman. David was dead proud of his watch, he kept stretching his arm so his cuff came up to show off his watch.

Lord Harris said, 'That's a nice watch you've got there David,' and David replied, 'Yes, I bought it today.' Lord Harris went on, 'Let me have a look at it,' so David took it off and handed it to him.

'Is it real then David?' he asked, and David said, 'Of course it is!'

'It will be waterproof then, won't it?' he asked as he dropped it into a pint of beer. Well, the look on David's face! It wasn't waterproof, of course, it was a fake. It kept going for about another week and that was the end of it.

Every morning we got up at six o'clock and after breakfast we went to the stables and worked the horses, getting them ready for the Team Competition.

We were there for ten days before the opening ceremony which was an incredible experience, it was like nothing else on earth. We even managed to see some of the athletics. I remember sitting right next to the trackside for the Men's 100m Final featuring Ben Johnson and Carl Lewis. Walking back through the Village in the evening one of the athletes was chatting to us and asked, 'So, what do you think of Ben Johnson?' We replied, 'Oh, he was brilliant wasn't he?' Nobody had told us that he had been disqualified!

When it came to the day of the Team Competition we didn't exactly startle, we didn't move any mountains, in fact, we didn't make much impression at all. By the time I jumped I was sick as a pig because I knew we wouldn't be getting a medal.

Ronnie, the eternal optimist, said to me, 'Don't worry, if

Jappeloup gets eliminated we can get Bronze.' I replied, 'He's about as likely to get eliminated as I am to fly to the moon.' Jappeloup was probably the best horse in the world at the time. We didn't get a medal of course, we finished sixth. Not disgraced, I suppose.

But now I was looking forward to the Individual, which was being held in the main Olympic Stadium, quite an honour.

We had a very early start and had to walk the course at six in the morning.

Ronnie came in to wake us up at five o'clock. He came out of his room shouting, 'Right then, come on you lads, this is the day you've been waiting for!' To which Michael, our reserve rider, replied, 'Why? Are we going home?'

Michael sat through the whole of the Seoul Olympics, three long weeks and he never got to jump. He was so good natured, so helpful, he never let it get him down, he was brilliant and in his quiet way he contributed enormously to the fun we were having.

As we were rushing around to get dressed and ready to go, all David was worried about was where he could pick up his packed lunch at five in the morning, so that he could eat it at the trackside between rounds. He wasn't worried about the course, or the fences to be jumped, just his lunch. If Ronnie had won the Gold for snoring, then the medal for eating would have to have gone to David.

It was still dark when we got down to the stadium so, basically, we walked the course in the dark. The floodlights were on, but they weren't daylight-bright, just a sort of twilight.

The course was huge, it was the biggest thing I had ever seen and by now I had been to a lot of international competitions. Walking into the stadium gave you an eery feeling. History would be made today.

In the first round, the last fence was a double; a triple bar with one stride to a vertical. Apollo had the back rail off the triple bar going in which was very uncharacteristic of him.

David was very unlucky; Countryman lost a shoe, slipped and had a plank down. David should have got a medal, he finished fourth. Apollo and I finished seventh. Not disgraced, I suppose.

CHAPTER EIGHTEEN
Major Wager

Paul Schockemöhle contacted me after the Olympics to tell me he had a fantastic horse for me. The horse was to be entered in the famous PSI Sale auction but Paul thought I should look at him first.

I went to Paul's stables where he told me, 'The horse is very, very careful but he needs a good rider, he's not an amateur ride.' The horse was called Landsturm, hurricane in German. I tried him in Paul's indoor school and the feeling he gave me over a fence was unbelievable. Like Paul said, he was very careful but didn't seem to have all the scope in the world.

Sarah went to the auction with Sally Mapleson to buy the horse. When we got him home I sold a half share to a friend of mine, Gary Widdowson, who used to ride in young riders.

The horse had a very good character. He had a lovely head on him and again, was a really kind horse. A more careful horse you couldn't hope to find. I am not exaggerating when I say that in the whole of his career, he maybe had five fences down. He was a truly remarkable horse. We renamed him Major Wager.

I remember the first show I took him to at Church Farm in Staffordshire. He didn't clear the fences by inches, he cleared them by feet. But he didn't like water. He really, really hated water. One day in Rotterdam he deposited me in the water jump. Stopped dead, and shot me over the bush, straight into the water.

From then on I didn't bother jumping Major outdoors. He was always much stronger outdoors, he was looking for the water, wondering if it would be the next fence, his mind wasn't on the job. So I jumped him indoors instead, where there was no open water. He didn't mind water trays, it was open water he disliked.

Over a period of time he became more scopey and ended up winning a World Cup Qualifier in Paris in 1993 and the Grand Prix in Gothenburg. But returning to Paris in 1994 was a disaster for Major Wager. Although he now had more scope, he was still jumping much higher than necessary over a fence. He fell victim to his own ability when he jumped a triple bar so high and landed so steeply that one of his front tendons gave way.

Major Wager spent months in Germany in an equine clinic before coming home to convalesce, but he was never able to jump again and had to be retired. He is still in the village and lives just three doors away with Alison and David Coleman who use him as their hack. They really love him and he is very happy.

It goes in three's

It was Horse-of-the-Year-Show time of year and we were off to Wembley again. Those of you who have visited the Horse of the Year Show will know how the stabling complex is set up. The stables are all outside and there is a sand working-in arena in the middle of the stabling.

In this particular year we were allocated stables that overlooked the sand arena. This meant our horses had lots to look at and there was plenty going on, they would never be bored. However, for Airbourne, who was well on his way to becoming a top-class horse, it was a disaster.

One of the classes at Wembley is the Police Horse of the Year. For this class the horses are subjected to the type of scenes they might have to face in the course of their duties. Each day, the police horses and their riders practised out in the sand arena, complete with a mini 'demonstration', balloons, crowds shouting, firecrackers, and to top it all, a fiery burning hoop through which the horses were expected to jump. For the police horses, of course, this is regular, run-of-the-mill, everyday stuff. They must experience worse than this at a football match or in a riot situation.

Bu all this was taking place only a few yards from Airbourne's stable door and he became very agitated. At around lunchtime he started to colic. The show vet was called, a 'nervous colic' was diagnosed and an injection administered. Mark Beever, my groom, walked the horse near enough all day long. Every couple of hours the vet would come back and check the horse and, when necessary, give him another injection.

Towards the end of the day Airbourne was in such a lot of pain that he tried to lie down and roll on the concrete path while Mark was leading him around. The injections were not controlling the pain. The vet then decided that the horse would have to go to the Royal Veterinary College at Potters Bar for treatment. A horsebox took Airbourne there at about 9 p.m., with Mark standing in the back to stop him lying down on the journey. Airbourne was put in a stall, examined and it was decided that they would have to operate. Mark returned to Wembley in the early hours of the morning with the news that Airbourne had come through the operation well.

Airbourne was still in the clinic at Potters Bar when we arrived home from the Show to find Full Cry, a good young horse of my own, suffering from colic. His condition deteriorated and he was sent for an operation, too. Full Cry recovered but I couldn't believe it was possible to have two horses operated on for colic inside a week and I arranged to send all the hay, feed and shavings back to the manufacturers. We changed everything except the water.

After a couple of days Airbourne seemed to have recovered and was sent home from the clinic to Sally Mapleson's to recuperate from his ordeal. But it was not to be and about ten days later he went back to Potters Bar for a second operation from which he never recovered. They discovered that the food he'd eaten was just lying there at the bottom of his stomach, it was almost as if his digestive system had completely packed in.

I was in 's-Hertogenbosch when the news reached me that Airbourne had died in the operating theatre at the veterinary college. It was devastating news for all of us connected with the horse but especially for Sally Mapleson. Not only had she lost a lovely horse destined for a great future but a couple of months earlier she had turned down a lot of money for Airbourne. Sally had never owned such a good horse before and she had decided that she would prefer to keep him and enjoy his success herself.

After losing J Nick I had wondered who the 'three' would be and now I knew. I had lost two good horses in J Nick and Airbourne and very nearly lost a third, Full Cry. Surely that was the end of my run of bad luck, I thought. Wrong again.

A couple of months later, Fred Harthill sent me a horse called Pennwood Fleetline. Mick Saywell's son Andrew was working for me and one day he was working it in the indoor school. Suddenly, there was a loud crash. I went running in and the horse was dead on the floor. He had had a heart attack.

Now I had lost three horses. See? These things always go in three's.

Apart from winning the Derby, 1988 was a bad year for me but it finished on a good note when my second son Harry was conceived over the New Year.

Swap shop

For the whole of that winter, Apollo had a good rest. I thought the Olympics might have taken a lot out of him, what with the long journey and everything. He lived outdoors in a warm rug and loved it. He really did prefer being in the paddock to being in the stable, it suited his outdoor mentality. So he was fresh as a daisy when the start of the '89 season came. We kicked off in the sunshine at Rome and then won a third successive Team Gold Medal at the European Championships in Rotterdam, followed by my third Hickstead Derby victory.

Tony Elliot was still on a buying spree and bought me three more young horses: Bluebird, which we bought from Mick Saywell and later on went on to win the Hickstead Derby with John Popely; Governor; and Destiny. My yard was almost full of Tony's horses. But out of them all, Apollo, Grand Slam, Serenade and Major Wager were the main contenders.

I decided on a spending spree of my own and set about building indoor stabling on the side of the indoor school. Carey Sage, together with his brother Austin, spent months at Sandall House Farm and made a terrific job of the building, especially the drainage. The land at Sandall House Farm was mainly peat and very wet in the winter. But at least the land never became hard in the summer, so I was able to use a small paddock on the other side of the stream for jumping. I built water ditches, dykes, banks, pretty much everything the horses could reasonably be expected to meet in competition.

The indoor stabling complex boasted a wash-box with hot running water and heat lamps for drying the horses, together with a feed room and office. It was very high so that hay and feed could be stored over the stables. The stables that were attached to the house were knocked down and the house extended. Now it felt like a house instead of a cottage.

I bought my first good car, a BMW 5-Series from Alan Kerr who cut me a deal and provided a sponsored Daihatsu Fourtrak for the use on the yard. My spending spree was going well.

Then I decided to try a spot of bartering instead of spending. One day I was riding one of my own horses, Attraction, around the collecting ring at Hickstead. I was chatting to John Whitaker who was on a mare called Florida. We were just walking around, talking, when I suddenly turned to him and said, 'I'm really sick of this horse, it's just not doing what it should be doing.'

John replied, 'I'm sick of mine as well, I can't get her going, she's always stopping.'

'Do you fancy a swap then?' I asked him and he said, 'Yeah, why not?'

So he got off, I got off, we swapped horses and off we went up to Ring Three to jump. By now, everybody had heard what we had done and they all rushed over to watch what would happen.

John jumped a clear round on my horse Attraction and I went into the ring on Florida and couldn't get through the start. It was like being back on Maybe. John was second in the class with my horse and he came up to me afterwards and said, 'Listen, I feel a bit guilty, that mare really can throw it in, I'll swap back if you like.'

But, like a fool, I said, 'No, a deal's a deal. I'll stand by it.' I should have known better than to think I could take a horse that was stopping with John and expect it to go for me. I didn't bother trying to jump Florida again that week, I simply put her on the lorry and took her home where I set about working her, with the help of my brother Michael. We spent all afternoon trying to persuade her to cross the bridge over the stream at the bottom of the field so we could get to the jump paddock. Finally, we got her there and she jumped well. Afterwards, I put her on the lorry and took her to a little local show at the Offchurch polo grounds where there was a Small Open. I pulled her straight off the lorry with her tack on, jumped her in the Open and she won it.

At the end of the year Florida was going really well so I gave her to Sarah to ride and together they won the Grade C Final at the Horse of the Year Show in 1990. After that, I took the ride back from Sarah and Florida went on to win the Grand Prix in Arnhem in June 1991, beating John into second place with Gammon. I had got a good deal in the swap after all. I wasn't really surprised, often a horse will jump for one rider but not for another. After winning the Grand Prix in Arnhem she went on to win the Grand Prix in Zuidlaren and Leeuwarden.

Top Gun

Government changes to the rules on cigarette advertising rendered the Raffles sponsorship contract null and void because we couldn't use the prefix, so I lost the sponsorship early. Fortunately, Mick Saywell did me a big favour in introducing me to Steve Spouge who arranged sponsorship with Burmah Castrol. The deal was for three years and the horsebox was re-sprayed in the corporate colours of Burmah Castrol.

Throughout the turmoil of all the building work and the house extension, poor Sarah was pregnant and on 20 September, Harry, my second child, was born. Sarah again surrendered herself to the mercies of Solihull Hospital and the birth went well, but there were other problems that upset her.

I had been doing a bit of business with Mick Saywell who told me he knew where there was a very good seven-year-old, right here in England. The horse was up in Yorkshire with Carl and Mark Fuller. Mick was convinced that it was as good a horse as he had ever seen and I phoned Tony Elliot who said he thought the horse belonged to Paul Schockemöhle. I spoke to Paul and he told me the horse was returning to Germany so he could assess its potential and that if I wanted to try it I would have to go to his yard at Muhlen.

Sarah was due to give birth any day now and I was already committed to compete at Bremen. Although it made sense to combine the two trips I didn't really want to have to go over to Germany any earlier than necessary but Mick insisted, 'Whatever you do, go and buy it.'

Bremen was scheduled for 21– 24 September and the horses were already on their way. On Tuesday 19th I drove over to Muhlen and tried the horse on Wednesday 20th. Its name was Top Gun. As soon as I sat on it I knew Mick Saywell was right, the horse was every bit as good as he had told me. But that very same day Sarah went into labour and Harry was born while I was trying the horse. Even though I had been due to go abroad on the 21st, anyway, Sarah never forgave me for going to buy a horse when she was due to give birth.

Gary Widdowson came with me to Paul's, looking for a young horse. When Gary saw Top Gun jump he immediately said that he wanted to buy the horse himself, for me to ride. With 20/20 hindsight I should have let him, Gary was a good owner and already had two horses with me. If I had known what was around the corner, I would have let Gary buy it. But instead I said, 'No, you can't buy Top Gun. I came out here for Tony Elliot and he's got first take on the horse. I wouldn't do that to Tony, he's been very good to me.'

I phoned Tony and told him how good the horse was, that it was the best horse I had ever seen and he bought it for me to ride. Johnny Wrathall, my friend from the old days, was driving the horsebox for me and he collected Top Gun on the way home from the show at Bremen.

I flew home to a new son, a new horse and a load of grief from Sarah ...

The first thing I wanted to do was to get my new star out. The following weekend was a Talent Spotters Final at Stoneleigh. I went there and in his first class Top Gun jumped three clear rounds and won the final. At seven years of age he was capable of jumping big tracks but personally I don't think jumping too big a track at a young age is good for the mind of a horse. Maybe they can, but they shouldn't be asked to. I say, don't push them, it can ruin them. People try and do too much with a seven-year-old and they pay for it later. When horses get past eight or nine years old, as long as you can keep them sound then you can keep them going until they are sixteen or so, because their mind stays confident. It's all in the mind and it's all about confidence.

So Top Gun competed in the smaller classes as third horse at international shows. He was an amazing horse, he had tremendous scope. When you jumped him it didn't really matter if you were six inches too close, or six inches too far off, as long as you were somewhere within the vicinity of the fence he could jump it.

Jet black, 16.2 hands, by Grannus of the famous 'G'-line, Top Gun was a character. He would look at things and see gremlins. He was a bit spooky when I first got him; sometimes he would turn and run the other way. The first day I rode him I had a job to get him up the field, just like Florida. Top Gun saw something in the hedge, reared up and whipped round. We had a bit of a disagreement but after that there was never a problem.

After Bremen, Apollo was rested. He didn't do much indoors through the winter. Grand Slam and Serenade were numbers one and two, and Top Gun was third horse. Apollo had won the gold at the Europeans, he'd done his bit. He deserved a break.

CHAPTER NINETEEN

Grand Slam

Grand Slam was a lovely, easy horse. At 16 hands he wasn't over big and he was quite thoroughbreddy. Like Top Gun, he was by Grannus. He was a beautiful model of a horse, with a very kind temperament. My son Daniel was only five years old but he could ride Grand Slam around the yard, he was so good natured. Daniel could even trot and canter him around the indoor school. Grand Slam had beautiful manners, he was very balanced, and he only wanted to please. When Tony Elliot first bought him for me he didn't have all the ability in the world but he improved over the years.

One year at Amsterdam they had a Masters. I had qualified with Grand Slam but that sort of pure power-jumping didn't really suit him; although he was very careful, he was not the scopiest of jumpers. There were seven of us and we had to make the draw in the ring. I thought there was no way I would win it and by the time my name came out of the hat the worst draw I could get was fourth; so I simply chose to go fourth in each round.

The Masters is a unique class in that the winner takes all. There is no prize money for second or third. It is fault and out, and each rider who jumps clear nominates a fence to be raised, or widened, immediately before they jump their next round. Obviously, each rider raises a fence which he thinks his horse will be able to jump, but hopes that it will catch out the opposition when it comes to their round.

Grand Slam jumped clear in the first round, each rider who jumped clear put up a fence, and then we jumped clear in the next round. A couple of riders dropped out. I kept putting up the planks, the last fence. I was going for careful jumping, not scope. As the rounds progressed the other riders all faulted and were out, leaving only myself with Grand Slam trying his heart out, and Hervé Godingon riding Guidam du Revelle. Hervé's horse was a successful breeding stallion and had much more ability than little ole' Grand Slam.

Hervé had the better draw and I knew there was no way I was going to beat him. I figured that the only way of me getting any money out of this class was to try and do a deal with Hervé. I knew in my own heart there was no way Grand Slam would out jump Guidam so I made an offer to Hervé, 'If I pull out, will you split the prize money with me?' 'No way,' he replied.

So Grand Slam went in again and jumped clear; then Hervé and Guidam jumped clear. I went to Hervé again and said, 'Come on, the lights are flashing on the dashboard, I'm in the red, I'm at my wits' end, let's do a deal,' but again, he replied, 'No.'

We went back in the ring and again I put the plank up; it was about six feet high now. Grand Slam was incredible and jumped his heart out and went round clear. Each time he had gone in, Hervé had put up the oxer coming out of the double; he was going for scope, not careful. The double was just before the planks and again, Hervé put the double up, but he had so much pace as he landed over the oxer that he had the plank down! Grand Slam and I had won. I didn't know whether I was more pleased at winning the £11,000 or seeing Hervé lose, having twice offered him a deal for me to retire!

How Grand Slam jumped that oxer coming out of the double I don't know. He walked up the front rail, scrambled across it and came down the other side. All without knocking a pole down. Amazing.

An empty yard

Jan Tops, the Dutch rider and one of the biggest horse dealers in the world at that time, had come to stay overnight with Sarah and me, en route to Birmingham Airport the next morning. At about nine o'clock at night, the phone rang and it was Tony Elliot. He dropped a bomb shell on me. He told me that all his horses were for sale because he had a tax problem. All nine of them. And the horsebox. This included Grand Slam, the brilliant Top Gun, Serenade, all my top horses with the exception of Apollo who would be my only good horse left, apart from Major Wager and Fiorella, a speed horse owned by Gary Widdowson.

Tony continued, 'I need you to sell them all, within the week.' It seems he needed a vast sum of money, quickly. Tony told me how much he wanted for the lot, and offered me a small percentage commission. I thought that was big of him, considering I had just built them up into one of the top strings in the world. I wouldn't be left with much after he took my livelihood away from me, after all the work I had done.

I was utterly devastated, absolutely shell-shocked. I didn't stay on the phone to him for very long. I couldn't believe what I was hearing. I bitterly regretted not letting my good mate Gary Widdowson buy Top Gun.

I told Jan Tops what had transpired on the telephone, that I had to sell virtually all my horses within the week. Jan asked which horses were for sale, and for how much. At the price Tony had quoted to me, he was making a good profit on what he had paid for them.

I convinced Jan that in Top Gun, I had possibly the best horse in the world on my yard so the next morning Jan tried him. We went back into the house and talked it over. Jan offered to buy all nine horses, and the horsebox, and he gave me three months to find another buyer for them who would let me keep the rides. This was very generous of Jan. Using me as the go-between, he and Tony then haggled about the price for a while, but finally a deal was struck. In order for Jan to get the lowest possible price, I had thrown in my commission as a deal. Now I had just three months to find buyers for the horses in order to keep them in my own yard, otherwise, all I would have left would be Apollo, who was getting towards the twilight of his career, Fiorella a good speed horse, Major Wager and young Florida, my swapshop horse.

I set about trying to find a buyer for the nine horses, the lorry was the least of my problems. I rang round everybody I could think of in England who might buy a horse for me. I contacted David

Broome in case Lord Harris wanted to buy them, or some of them, or even just one of them. The one I really wanted to keep was Top Gun. He was definitely going to be one of the best horses in the world. I called Michael Bates, Michael Bullman, Ronnie Massarella. I even tried to get a syndicate together but nothing came of it. No one would, or could, buy them.

I had become very friendly with Ludger Beerbaum in the days when we were buying horses through Paul Schockemöhle and he was a good friend to me. I called Ludger and told him my problem. He had a very good sponsor at the time called Mr Moxell. Ludger offered to speak with his sponsor, but sadly nothing came of it. Jan, being a dealer, needed profit on these horses and Mr Moxell wasn't interested.

Then Jan had another idea; he suggested that if I couldn't find a buyer within the three months then we would sell them individually for as much money as possible and split the profit. I decided that wasn't too bad, at least I would earn some money out of it all.

The season was just starting, so I set off to the World Cup shows with the horses, all of them owned now by Jan Tops. In 's-Hertogenbosch Top Gun won the Grand Prix. People on the circuit knew the situation and there was a lot of interest in the horses but I wasn't doing very well finding a buyer for myself, I 'd virtually given up. Now my main efforts were to try and sell them for as much as possible and split the profit with Jan.

The horses were now priced individually, they were no longer for sale as a package deal. On the way to the World Cup final in Dortmund we were stabled with Axel Wockener in Germany where the American rider Debbie Dolan tried Top Gun. But she didn't buy him. I expect she has regretted that many times since then.

At the World Cup final Top Gun won the Grand Prix, he was definitely realising his potential. And believe it nor not, Grand Slam won the second leg of the World Cup final, beating Milton! Although Milton went on to win the final and Jappeloup was second. Grand Slam and I finished sixth overall.

To cut a long story short, Jan Tops quietly arranged to sell Top Gun to his own sponsor, Alfonso Romo, and would be keeping the ride for himself. Jan also arranged to sell Governor to Phillipe

Lejeune in Belgium and the horse went on to win two Mercedes Masters in Stuttgart; Blue Bird was sold to John Popely and went on to win the Hickstead Derby; Serenade was sold to Martin Lucas and became his best horse; they truly were a top string of horses. The remaining horses all went to Holland to Jan's dealing yard.

With all the horses gone, I came home from Dortmund with an empty horsebox. Jan told me that the horses had been sold for no more than he had paid for them, there was no profit to be split with me. I found that hard to believe, but at least I had the horsebox.

Back home at Sandall House Farm, the situation was very tough. I had hardly any horses and no money; it was all invested in the property. I wasn't the easiest person to be living with and this put a strain on my marriage.

In May, Jan told me that Grand Slam had not yet been sold. Sarah and I talked it over and then had a meeting with our bank manager at Barclays. We arranged to mortgage the farm to raise the money to buy Grand Slam. This was not a very wise thing to do, but I had my back against the wall, I had to do something, I needed another good horse on the yard. We insured Grand Slam for the price we paid, and also took out a life assurance policy on my life so that the mortgage would be paid off if anything should happen to me.

Grand Slam turned out to be a very good buy. At the 1990 World Championships in Stockholm he was on the British team with Milton, Monsanta and Countryman. Between the four of them they carried John Michael, David and myself to a Bronze Medal. Grand Slam really was improving with age and that year he won £60,000; that helped pay towards the mortgage.

Johnny Wrathall, one of the three musketeers, had been driving my horsebox whenever he had the chance. He enjoyed coming to shows, and I enjoyed having him there, he was good company. Johnny had driven the horses out to Lucerne, Rome, all over Europe.

About two weeks before we were due to leave for the World Championships in Stockholm, Johnny called me. He had time off and wasn't busy, could he drive me? I told him I didn't need him as my horses were going with John Whitaker and he already had a driver. Instead, Johnny got a job driving for David Rogers Transport at Northampton; they were looking after Madonna who was singing at Wembley Stadium. David Rogers is a good supporter of show jumping and nearly always comes to the World Cup Final and the Championships.

Anyway, Johnny was hired to drive all Madonna's equipment from Wembley to Paris the night after the concert. It was arranged that Johnny would drive from London to Paris with another driver. Johnny drove to the ferry and they swapped over in Calais. Tragically, the other driver fell asleep at the wheel while John was taking a nap in the bunk at the rear of the cab. They hit a bridge and were both killed. In a way, I have always felt a bit responsible for Johnny dying. If only I had let him drive my horses in my lorry, he would still be with us today.

Phoenix Park

In June my luck took a turn for the better when David Broome offered me his good horse Phoenix Park to ride. Phoenix Park had been plagued with injury throughout his career and by the time he came to me he only had one lung – as a result of a nasty bout of pleurisy and pneumonia, and a carbon fibre implant in one of his front tendons. Caring for him was a real challenge and my groom Mark Beever rose to the challenge. Phoenix Park was fourteen years old, an Irish horse, grey, quite big at 17 hands, by Hildenly. He hadn't jumped much having had two years off with his lung problems. With only one lung and three good legs you would think he had had enough trauma in his life, but there was more to come.

Phoenix Park was an odd horse. He never lay down. He used to go to sleep standing up and would then fall over. His staying mechanism can't have been working properly. You would often hear a big crash in the stable and there he would be, down on the floor. But he had a nice soft landing; he was always bedded down on paper because having just the one lung his respiratory system was very delicate.

Immediately I struck up a good relationship with him. If he hadn't been plagued with injury he could have been one of the great horses. He had an enormous jump and was very careful but he was difficult to sit on over a fence. When he landed he would often anticipate the next turn and make a left or a right before you were ready. And sometimes he would guess wrong and go the wrong way.

He nearly unshipped me once at Wembley but he actually did get David on the floor in Paris during the World Cup. It was at a combination; he jumped in and unshipped David as he landed. David came off and was sitting with his back to the second element, an oxer. Phoenix Park kept going, all on his own, and jumped straight over the top of David, and the fence, and then jumped the third element!

I rode him in one show at Franconville on the outskirts of Paris and then took him straight to Dublin where he won the Grand Prix. The following year he won the Grand Prix again.

From getting the ride on him in June through to Olympia in December of 1990 he won near enough £100,000. At the end of the year, David Broome and I couldn't agree on the prize money split. He wanted more than me. Sometimes owners have disagreements with their riders about the prize money split. The late Malcolm Barr, John Whitaker's father-in-law, once suggested to John that he thought they should have a different arrangement the next year. 'Why?' asked John. 'Do you want to ride the horse?' Apparently Mr Barr never raised the subject again.

I told David that I wasn't prepared to go on riding Phoenix Park under his terms so the next season the horse was sent to the Edgars and Marie had a go at riding him but it wasn't a successful partnership. Sure enough, David knew which side his bread was buttered and Phoenix Park arrived back in my yard in July.

He immediately started winning again. We won the Kerrygold Grand Prix in Dublin, were fourth in the Grand Prix in Rotterdam, had a good show at Spruce Meadows in Calgary and took a Team Silver in La Baule at the European Championships. To finish off, he won the Masters at the Horse of the Year Show.

And then he finished himself off. After returning home on the Sunday morning he was turned out in the paddock when I heard an almighty crash on the outside wall of the indoor school. I ran to have a look and found Phoenix Park standing there with his hind leg swinging. The metal sheeting of the school was bent a foot inwards he had hit it with such force.

He was led in on three legs, one hind leg swinging round and round. I rang David to warn him that we would probably have to put the horse down, as he appeared to have broken his leg.

My vet , John Williams, lives in the village and he rushed over and diagnosed a broken tendon down the front of the hock. Phoenix Park was taken to John's Avonvale equine clinic where the injury was judged to be inoperable. I wanted the horse to have a chance though, so I telephoned the brilliant German vet, Dr Peter Cronau, and he flew over and operated on the tendon. He threaded eighteen inches of carbon fibre down the centre of the tendon, attaching it each end at the tendon insert. Clever stuff.

Phoenix Park came home to recover but within a week he developed colic. Watching him trying to get down to roll but unable to because of his newly repaired hind leg was one of the worst sights of my life. He ended up back at the Avonvale Clinic where he had another operation. That's when I gave him the name Bionic Horse.

Amazingly, he made a full recovery from all of this and finished his days happily jumping with local Warwickshire rider David Austin.

CHAPTER TWENTY
In the Park

The Burmah Castrol arrangement ceased, leaving me without a sponsor again. I feared there would be lean times ahead but in the summer of 1990 Mike Rowland from Alan Paul Hairdressing offered to sponsor Geoff Billington and me. The Alan Paul colours were very pretty – pink, white and grey. The saddle cloths were white with pink writing and the bandages were pink. Jackets were grey with pink and white writing.

The whole effect wasn't very macho but we got used to it eventually. The horsebox was painted up in the Alan Paul livery and looked quite startling as it went along the roads. I think it was one of the first horseboxes to be painted pink and the colour has since become quite popular.

Mike Rowland rode at a lower level so he understood horses – he was a good laugh was Mike. Alan Paul were great sponsors but unfortunately Mike and his partner Alan Moss got into a bit of trouble and had to wind the company up. Mike was very good about it, he told us what had happened and the sponsorship ceased after about eighteen months.

But there were no hard feelings, we didn't fall out over it and Geoff and I took Mike Rowland to Kossen skiing later on in January 1992. We competed at the snow show in Kossen every year and always combined it with a spot of skiing. Mike had never skied before but Geoff and I told him that the best way to learn was to go up to the top of the mountain, put your skis on and just come down nice and gently.

Mike obediently put his skis on and straight away he fell over. Geoff started laughing and I said to Mike, 'Come on, we'll ski down a bit and then you follow us.' He looked at us doubtfully. 'And then we'll wait for you and when you catch up we'll go on again,' I assured him. I could see him thinking, 'Yeah, right,' but Geoff and I set off down the slope. We stopped after a couple of hundred yards and we could see Mike coming down, he was doing pretty well considering. But there was a group of beginners, all stood in a line, and as Mike skied towards them – seemingly in control, but actually not – he shouted, 'Watch out!' and promptly wiped out about six of them.

Geoff and I were dying of laughter, we were splitting our sides, killing ourselves laughing. I said, 'Come on Geoff, he's gonna be all day let's get on.' So we left him lying in the middle of the ski class and shot off down the slopes. We were in a bar drinking gluhwein about two hours later when we saw this person in the distance, walking along with his skis on his shoulder and falling over every ten yards. It was Mike. When he finally arrived at the bottom, he complained, 'You're a nice pair leaving me like that,' so I said, 'Well now you know what it feels like when you left us!'

Not long afterwards, Mike and Alan's 'bit of trouble' escalated and they both spent some time in one of Her Majesty's hostelries. Tragically, Alan died very soon after he was released. He was a lovely man, it was terribly sad, I think the stress was all too much for him.

It's a wild place though, Kossen; Hannes Stern, the lad that runs the snow show, has some great parties in his little family-run hotel, the Gasthof Post. I went there for three or four years on the trot.

One year I took Richard Dunwoody with me. He had been banned for three weeks for pushing Adrian Maguire off the track at Nottingham (!) and he was completely fed up and bored, so he came on holiday with me. We shared a room and had some wild nights. He thought the jockeys knew how to have a good time but we show jumpers definitely held our own!

Another time, Geoff Billington, Michael Whitaker and I ended up in the same bed. I have no idea why. It's a good job I only went there once a year, I needed a rest when I got home. And one year Chris Goosen threw up in my suitcase. I was sharing a room with Chris and when I woke up in the morning and went to open my suitcase, Chris had been sick in it. Charming!

Clean living

Chris Goosen's son, Guy, was a useful young rider. He had come up through pony ranks and it was time for him to move on to horses. Despite having been sick in my suitcase, when Chris asked me to have Guy work on my yard for the winter, I said yes. Guy was a lovely lad, some of the best times at Sandall House Farm were when Guy was there.

He moved in at the beginning of the winter and had to sleep on a bed shoved in a corner somewhere. He didn't have a proper bedroom, we were very short of staff accommodation. I think Guy had been pampered a bit. He certainly wasn't an easy man to get out of bed in the morning. He liked his bed.

Every morning he turned up late on the yard, so in the end, five minutes after he was supposed to be on the yard, I opened his door and slung a bucket of water over him. Apparently it took days for his mattress to dry out, especially as I am very frugal with the central heating!

Because he was always in such a rush to get up in the morning, Guy also had a habit of turning up on the yard unshaven. I used to tell him to get a shave before he came out. Sometimes he did, sometimes he didn't. One night we had been to a show at Stoneleigh and got back quite late. We did the horses off and then five minutes later Guy came over to the house and said, 'See you later, I'm just going out.' I assumed he was going to see his girlfriend at the time, Emma White.

I asked, 'Aren't you gonna have a shower before you go out and a shave?' Guy said, 'No, I'll do that when I get back.' I persevered, 'Have a shower before you go out,' after all, poor Emma White wouldn't want him unshaven would she? But Guy insisted, 'No, no, I'll be all right, I'll have one when I get back.'

Chris had told me to be quite hard on Guy, the lad wasn't really spoilt, he was just very easy going. 'You're not going out unless you get showered and shaved. Otherwise you are stopping in,' I told him. Guy caved in. 'All right then I'll go and do it.' But I had had a bright idea. I would cure him permanently of going out unwashed.

'If you wanna go out, just so as you'll remember every time in future, you've got to shower in the horse washroom, where the horses are. Then you will remember to shower before you go out, every time.' Guy had no choice. I often grounded him for minor misdemeanours. If he did something wrong, or if the tack wasn't clean enough he would either be grounded or he would have to clean the toilets.

Anyway, sure enough, in the middle of winter, Guy goes off down the yard to the horses' washbox. I threw him a bar of soap and a towel and shut the door on him. Ten minutes later, Simon Gatward, who was working for us, went down to the stables and opened the washbox door to see how Guy was getting on. He had switched on all the solarium lights used to dry the horses and was having a nice cosy, warm shower. Simon promptly took a photograph of him; if you've still got it Simon, send us a copy!

After that, Guy never forgot to take a shower, at least, not while he was with me. Guy had a lot of success with Gary Widdowson's horse, Fiorella, my former ride and he now works for Paul Schockemöhle in Germany with his sister Mandy, another good rider.

A golden opportunity

Driving home from a Kossen skiing holiday in January 1991, Sarah and I were waiting for the ferry when the phone rang; it was Freddie Welch. He told me that his wife Sue was going to call and ask me to ride a horse of hers called Glint of Gold.

Freddie explained, 'Sue's got a big chestnut horse she wants you to have. I know it's not very careful but whatever you do, don't be horrible about it because she thinks the world of it, it's a pet. But if you take that one and get on with it for a while you're sure to get another one.'

He was absolutely right and a bit later on, Sue rang me up. 'Would you like to have Glint of Gold?' she asked me and I thought, 'Well, not really,' but I said, 'I'd be delighted.' Thanks for warning me Freddie!

Sue was one of my better owners in that she understood horses, that they aren't machines but have to be carefully nurtured. Sue rode herself and was Ladies European Champion many moons ago. She came to me as an owner in 1991 and still has a horse with me that my son Daniel rides.

If I were able to have a second mother I would choose Sue, as you wouldn't find a nicer person anywhere in the world. She has been with me now for ten years and in the last years I don't know what I would have done without her. Sue has supplied me with some very good horses and I wouldn't be where I am today without her support. I know I can pick up the phone at any time of the day and rely on her. Not only with show jumping, though. Sue also has a few good racehorses and in the wintertime we go racing a lot together. It's a good friendship.

When Glint of Gold arrived I found he could kick poles better than Kevin Keegan could kick footballs. I had the horse for a few months before finally Freddie and I persuaded Sue to get rid of the horse and buy something better.

We went to Paul Schockemöhle and bought a horse called Just Blackie, the first of many horses Sue bought for me. In later years, Sue bought Werra and Limited Edition and then at the 1991 PSI Sale she acquired Showtime who competed in the Olympics at Atlanta in 1996. It's a pity that Sue wasn't around as an owner when I had the chance of buying Top Gun. She is not the sort of person who would sell a horse from underneath you, you would know you have the horse for life.

Werra arrived at the yard in September 1991. She was an older, more experienced horse and was quite a difficult character, very strong to ride but an excellent jumper, so careful. She wasn't super sound, she was already twelve when Sue sent her to me; Werra was bought as a back-stop to keep me going. She did exactly that and won a couple of Grand Prix in Stuttgart and Hanover before retiring in 1992 and going back to Schockemöhle's to breed.

Limited Edition won a lot of good classes for me but was plagued with unsoundness. He won thirty-three classes from 1992 through to 1995 and a total of nearly a quarter of a million pounds. Like Apollo, Limited Edition was very versatile, he won Puissance, Speed Classes, Grand Prix and the Kings Cup at Hickstead.

Showtime, by Pilot, was only six years old and had had a foal by embryo transfer before she came to me. At only six I didn't jump her hard to start with.

The game's up

Unusually for me, that year I was taking two holidays. Having already been to Kossen skiing, in February Sarah and I flew out to Mauritius along with John and Clare Whitaker, David and Liz Broome and a group of other foreign riders. We were to combine a holiday with competing on borrowed horses at the Mauritius Horse Show.

One day, we lads were all due to go off together for a golf tournament and the women were staying behind on the beach to sunbathe and swim. I had a bad feeling about this and told John that I didn't fancy going off for the day, I didn't like the idea of leaving all those women on the beach, gossiping. 'It's not a good thing,' I complained, but John insisted, 'No, no, it'll be all right, come on.'

So we went off to play golf but when we arrived back at the hotel my feelings of foreboding were getting worse. The beach was on a little island a short boat ride from the hotel. I climbed in to the boat to go out to the island and I could see Sarah coming down the beach towards the jetty. She was looking rather – well, she was striding out purposefully, let me put it that way. Even at that distance I could see there was a glint in her eye and it wasn't gold.

I turned to John, 'I told you we shouldn't have gone golfing.' I was worried. I had been hiding something for years.

Sarah met me on the jetty and took a swing at me, clawing my back. I jumped off the jetty into the sea and then she marched off and caught the boat back to the hotel. When I returned to our room I discovered she had thrown all my clothes into the ocean and she wouldn't let me back in the room. I had to spend the rest of the holiday with John and Clare, sleeping in their room. It was a bit cramped and I think Clare moved out and went and shared with Sarah.

Rumours had been going round the show jumping circuit for some time that I had been having an affair and Sarah suspected that the woman's name began with a 'B' and ended with an 'A'.

That day on the beach, Jean Claude Vangeenberghe's wife Bonita had been sunbathing on the sand when Sarah sat down next to her and asked, 'Are you having an affair with my husband?' Bonita, who was completely innocent, was very keen to clear her own name and obviously thought the best course of action was to name the culprit. 'No,' she allegedly replied, 'it's not me, it's Bettina you're after. Bettina Melliger.'

When we came home from Mauritius, Sarah had the bright idea of obtaining a printout of the numbers I was calling from my mobile phone. My airtime provider obliged and Sarah found Bettina's number on the print out. I had been calling her several times a day.

The game was up. The marriage was over. I changed my airtime provider.

My affair with Bettina was a real love affair and Sarah could not and would not tolerate it. I don't blame her. In July that year she left Sandall House Farm and went home to stay with her parents in Shropshire, taking the children, Daniel and Harry with her. It was the hardest day of my life seeing my kids going out of the yard, something I will never, ever forget. My secretary patted me on the shoulder and said, 'Don't worry, they'll be back.' I didn't know she was psychic.

TWENTY ONE

Grand National-Fit

We had a work-placement student from Moreton Morrell Agricultural College. Charlotte Scott was the only satisfactory student we ever had, she really could ride well, she was a natural.

Charlotte was riding the older horses, Phoenix Park and Apollo. She was a redhead but I never saw a flash of temper from her. I had told her to get Apollo 'Grand National-fit' for his last assault on the Hickstead Derby. I was planning to retire him from top-class competition later that year and it would be his last appearance at Hickstead. Charlotte took me at my word and gave him lots of long, slow canter work and walked him up and down the hills for hours, making him tremendously fit and strong. As an older horse, Apollo needed to be super-fit to cope with the gruelling Derby track.

He looked terrific when he was loaded up to go down to Hickstead, and sure enough he was super-fit. Apollo produced one of only two clear rounds and we went into the jump-off against Joe Turi and Vital. He leapt over the open water at a gallop and then I tried to check him for the upright of rails straight after. I was expecting him to be a bit tired and to come back to me easily but he wasn't remotely worn out and took the rails too fast, just clipping the top pole off. He was second but because it was his last Derby he was decked out in a garland of leaves and a fuss was made of him. He probably thought he had won! I hope so. I wanted him to go out at the top.

We moved on to Dublin later in August and I became convinced that I should retire him soon. Every year I had taken Apollo to

Dublin he had always won a class; the Grand Prix, a speed class, the Puissance, something. But after his exertions in the Derby he was struggling. He was sixteen years old and he was finding it difficult to win. It was just old age and wear and tear.

I had a word with his owner, Linda Jones, and told her that I thought he should retire. We went to the indoor show in Copenhagen in October and that was his last indoor show. I kept him up over the winter, we didn't turn him away, and I took him to Kossen where he jumped on the snow. It was a lot lower key for him and he enjoyed himself, he thought it was fun but after he came home I retired him. He had done enough.

His owner, Linda Jones came on the phone to me and suggested that we sell him as a Young Riders' horse. I was absolutely staggered. I was amazed that she would even consider letting the horse go on working hard having been such a good servant.

But Apollo wouldn't want to languish in the field so I asked my father if he thought my stepmother Janette would like to have him to hunt. Janette was delighted and Apollo went to live at Odnaull End Farm, grazing in the fields where I had started riding with Oxo.

When I told Linda Jones that I had given him to my stepmother to hunt she wanted to know how much my father would pay for Apollo as a hunter. I told her that there was no way she was going to have the last penny out of him. 'The horse doesn't owe you anything,' I said, 'Why can't you just leave him be and let him retire doing something he enjoys? You should be honoured to have owned a horse like that, let him have a good retirement.'

Linda put the phone down on me and I've never heard from her since.

A couple of years later, I borrowed Apollo to hunt and went out with my friend – and vet – John Williams, who was riding West Tip (winner of the Grand National with Richard Dunwoody). I couldn't hold one side of him and after half an hour I gave up. He used to be very well behaved with Janette and did everything she wanted from him. But as soon as I got back on him he was off again, he must have been reliving old memories.

Apollo is still going strong at twenty-six years old. He had four seasons hunting and is now in complete retirement, roaming around the farm. While standing at the side of the covert, he sprung a tendon off his hock and was never ridden again.

Banned

Young Rider Keith Doyle came to train with me at Sandall House Farm. Keith is from the south of England, he's a grand lad and I enjoyed training him. We went to Munich together in my lorry and jumped there for four days. I took Just Blackie and a couple of other young horses.

For the first three days it rained so badly that the Grand Prix was moved indoors as the ground was awash with water. Munich showground is a big affair and there was plenty of room. I jumped in the Grand Prix but even though I wasn't placed, Just Blackie was dope tested. I thought nothing of it because as far as I knew, the horse was clean.

We returned home and a month later I unexpectedly received a letter from the FEI telling me that the test had proved positive for Isoxuprine, which is a blood thinner, like aspirin. Isoxuprine is a banned substance and is used for horses that are unsound.

I immediately started scratching my head, wondering where the heck it could have come from. I asked Mark Beever who had no idea, it was something we had never used. I rang the BSJA and told them that I was completely innocent. I didn't even know what the stuff was, let alone used it.

I called Sue Welch who owned Just Blackie and explained to her what had happened and she was very understanding. She knew as well as I did that Blackie was not unsound. Then I wondered: did Keith have a horse on the drug? After all, he had been travelling with me, the horses were all in very close proximity. John Williams, my Vet, had told me that it took only a minute trace of the substance to show positive in a dope test – it could have been on a scoop, or a shared feed bucket, it was quite feasible that the Isoxuprine had come from such a source.

But Keith said, 'No,' he didn't think so. I was still very puzzled, but I had to prove my innocence.

Keith Doyle's vet at that time was Simon Knapp, who is also

Sue Welch's vet and they are very good friends. Sue asked Simon if he had supplied Keith with any Isoxuprine and Sue told me that Simon replied, 'Yes, there is one horse at Keith's yard that I treat with it.'

I employed a lawyer, Chris Hall from Cripps Harries Hall. Chris sometimes commentated at the Horse of the Year Show so he had some knowledge of horses. When I told Chris the story he suggested that I ask Peter Doyle, Keith's father, if they had used Isoxuprine, or had a horse on it at home. Peter Doyle told me that he had never heard of the stuff, he didn't know anything about it. All I needed from him was a letter to say that he had a horse back at home that had been treated with the drug and that it had been accidentally misplaced; then I would be off the hook.

But Peter Doyle categorically denied any knowledge of the substance. Meanwhile, Keith was still training at my yard. Eventually he went home and Peter Doyle has never spoken to me from that day to this.

Subsequently, I ended up in Lausanne at the FEI headquarters and was banned for two months. I think I was fined £1,500. My solicitor's fees had been about £4,000. All to no avail.

I was competing at the Kossen and Cortina snow shows and inbetween the two shows I had the hearing at FEI headquarters. I drove from Kossen to Lausanne, which took hours across the mountains, just to get struck off. Because I was banned I couldn't then compete at Cortina so I let Guy Goosen ride Fiorella instead. She went well for him and he ended up buying her.

First words

Having lost the Alan Paul Hairdressing sponsorship, once again I was without a sponsor. I was in the collecting ring at the Maastrict show in November when the last person in the world I expected to help me marched straight up and asked, 'Do you want Everest back?' It was Ted Edgar. Those were the first words he had spoken to me since I had left back in 1985.

I was surprised that he had spoken to me at all, never mind to offer me a good sponsorship deal. I replied, 'Yeah, well, I haven't got a sponsor so I don't see any reason why not.'

A contract was thrashed out with the managing director, Kevin Mahoney, and Gerry Gregeen, who was in charge of PR for Everest. It was a generous sponsorship. I was now back on board with Everest. It was like having déjà vu.

The horsebox was repainted in the blue and green Everest colours and all the pink jackets, shirts and umbrellas were given away to friends. Smart new Everest ones took their place. All the horses had their prefixes changed yet again; back then, the horses names changed almost annually!

Everest were fantastic sponsors and we had some good times with Kevin Mahoney and Wayne Money, the deputy managing director. They were really interested in the sport, they followed it closely and were always on the rider's side. After taking me on, they also pulled on board John and Michael Whitaker. They were probably the biggest contributor to our sport in this country over the years, sponsoring classes as well as riders.

We always went to their Christmas parties at the Royal Lancaster Hotel. Over seven hundred people would attend. In February they would have a meeting of the 'Millionaires Club', a men-only night, for the members of their workforce who had done more than a million pounds' worth of business that year. That was always a good night out but I don't know what happened to the women who had done more than a million pounds' worth of business!

One night in particular springs to mind; John, Michael and I went down to London for a night out with Wayne and Kevin, together with a few other guys from Everest. We were in a bar and restaurant called Soho Soho, in Soho. We finished up very late and I took a taxi to the station where I got on a train to Coventry. But I fell asleep, missed my stop and had to turn round and come back from Birmingham in the early hours of the morning.

I thought that was a rough deal but John and Michael didn't get home until two days later. They had both had far too much to drink and couldn't possibly drive home. So Kevin and Wayne ordered a car transporter to take Michael's car home. Then they sent John and Michael home in a taxi, all the way to Nottinghamshire where

Michael lives. I don't think Veronique was very impressed when she saw the car arriving home before Michael! That's the sort of sponsors they were, so generous and good-hearted.

I'll never forget teaching Kevin Mahoney to ride. He wanted to learn to ride and have it on video so he could show off at the annual Everest awards. At that time the quietest horse in the yard was Dollar Girl so I taught him to ride on her. The first day was quite good, the second day was a bit better but then Kevin became ambitious and wanted to canter. He was in the school and went from trot to canter; Dollar Girl could tell that Kevin wasn't competent and she gradually built up speed and went round the corner of the school like a motorbike. Kevin fell, bounced off the wooden kicking boards at the side of the school, and ended up with splinters in his bum!

However, Kevin is a determined man and he was adamant that he was going to be filmed jumping on Dollar Girl; but I felt there was absolutely no way it was going to happen. In the end I filmed Kevin cantering around the corner to the fence, then I stopped filming, Kevin got off the horse and took the video camera from me, I got on, Kevin started filming, Dollar Girl jumped the fence with me and then I put Kevin back on board to continue around the school. We wore matching clothes and used very poor lighting. We showed the video at their promotional meeting and I think we got away with it.

I often still see Wayne and we go out now and again; at the Cheltenham Festival we always sit down and have a beer and chat about old times.

Visiting rights

I rarely sell a horse, but in 1992 I was approached by Torchy Millar, who asked if I would consider selling Grand Slam. He was now twelve years old and still a complete gentleman; he was ideal for a Young Rider. Fifteen-year-old Skye Eurilo came over from Canada to try him and loved him. He went beautifully for her and he was sold and went to live in Canada. Grand Slam had definitely proved a good buy, he had more than paid back the mortgage on the house. He jumped really well with Skye for several years before dying of a burst artery in his stomach.

Now that Sarah had moved out, every Monday was set aside to drive up to Shropshire to see Daniel and Harry. I used to collect them from school, bring them home for the night and then take them back the next morning. I received a hostile reception from Sarah, the reception was a bit like my old television: picture but no sound. For seven years, I religiously visited them, driving up to Shropshire like the old days when I was dating Sarah. The children would stay with me for school holidays, sometimes turning up complete with ponies.

Daniel had a chicken house at my farm. It was his hobby, he liked his chickens. He had all sorts of exotic breeds and in his holidays he would go to market with Janette's father, David Southall. He used to pick Daniel up and take him to Henley market every Wednesday. Daniel would set off with an empty crate and come back with a full one every time. He didn't rear chickens for eating like I used to, he just bought them, bought some more, hatched a few and then sold a few. David said that Daniel drove a really hard bargain at market even though he was only about ten years old.

One Christmas I bought Daniel and Harry a pair of reindeers. They were quite cute when they were fawns but they soon grew. After a while they became so big we had to build deer fencing around their paddock. We kept them for a few years but eventually sold them to a deer farm when they became much too big to handle.

CHAPTER TWENTY TWO

My Hospitality Knows No Bounds

Remember the lad who bundled me up in my sleeping bag and threw me out of the Edgars' horsebox many years back? Well, it was Olympic year and Tim Grubb came over from America for an attack at getting on the British team again. And guess where he based himself? Yep, at my house. I was his nanny.

He came over with Denizen, Two plus Two and another horse whose name escapes me. The long-suffering Fiona Scott was his groom and I seem to recall she slept in the feed room because we had run out of accommodation.

Tim and I didn't have a wife between us. Sarah had left me, and Tim's wife, Michelle McEvoy, was not happy with him and had stayed over in America.

The warning went out locally: 'Lock up your daughters!'

Tim lived as if he was staying in a hotel with a maid coming in every day. I would come down every morning to find all the lights on, the television still on and Johnny Walker lying dead on the floor! In the bathroom he left wet towels all over the floor. He had to use six towels when one would do. I had never seen anything like it. But Tim is good natured, he is very funny, he has an excellent sense of humour, and living with him, I soon developed one!

He used to get up at 12 noon, go outside and ask his groom to tack up his horses. She would refuse, telling him she'd already worked them and that I had ridden Denizen for him. So he would come back in and get some lunch. I think he was on holiday because by all accounts he works very long hours when he is in America.

151

Dollar Girl

Dollar Girl originally came into this country for John Whitaker to ride. Joe Haller, who owned the horse, always hung around John; he could usually be seen in the evening talking to John or having a drink with him. Joe was not the easiest of owners; he wasn't a horseman. Apparently, he had worked as a TV repairman before marrying well.

I had attended a birthday party for Joe Haller many years before at the Argentinian restaurant opposite the Martinez Hotel in Cannes. Joe had invited me along with John and Michael Whitaker and my Australian pal Jeff McVean. Swiss rider Thomas Fuchs was there with Willi and Bettina Melliger. Back then I had no idea that I would end up with two of the two best ladies in Switzerland – Bettina and Dollar Girl!

Joe wanted Dollar Girl to take part in the Barcelona Olympics but he wasn't getting on too well with the present rider, Thomas Fuchs. In order to compete at Barcelona, the horse would have to make the Swiss team.

At the Geneva show, late in '91, there was a bonus prize of 50,000 Swiss francs on offer for the horse that went through the show with no faults. By the end of the show, Dollar Girl was the only horse left that could win the bonus prize. She hadn't had a single fence down the whole time. Thomas Fuchs was in the jump-off for the Grand Prix but instead of playing safe with a steady clear, he tried to win the class as well as the bonus prize. Going fast against the clock, Dollar Girl had the last fence down and consequently didn't win the Grand Prix or the bonus prize.

Joe Haller threw his dolly out of the pram and promptly took the horse away from Thomas Fuchs, giving her to John to ride early in '92. John was his first choice of rider because it was assumed that Milton wouldn't be going to the Olympics, having missed Seoul in 1988.

John rode her in some of the World Cup Qualifiers but she didn't really suit his way of riding. In the meantime, it was confirmed that Mr and Mrs Bradley would let Milton go to Barcelona and that he would be John's intended mount. Dollar Girl was still left without a jockey for Barcelona and as the horse was registered to the British team, it was too late to change nationality. I did not have an Olympic horse, so John suggested that Joe give Dollar Girl to me to try. She had been off for a while with an abscess in her foot. I think she had probably had it for a long time, which is why she didn't go so well for John.

The first time I rode her was at Hickstead in the May meeting where they put a special Olympic Qualifier class on at the end of the show, after the Grand Prix. Having never sat on the horse before I had to go in this class; the mare had not arrived down at the ring soon enough and I only had about five minutes to warm up. It was an Olympic Qualifier and I had to get round with eight faults or less. Added to which, she had never been in the unique Hickstead arena before. For both of us, it was quite an ordeal but we managed to scrape through with only two fences down. At least I had qualified for Barcelona, although perhaps the worst thing I could have done was to qualify, bearing in mind what was to come later in the year.

I campaigned strongly with Dollar Girl and we jumped in Wolfsburg, Arnhem and Aachen. I had to try and get as much experience with her as I could. At Aachen we finished second in the Grand Prix to Jos Lansink on Egano. We then went on to Royan in France along with John, Tim, Michael and David; the five selected for the team at the Barcelona Olympics. David fell heavily at Royan and hurt his back, leaving him lame for a few days. Ronnie had five top horses and riders, but would only need four in the team. Who would he drop? The tension in the camp was so tangible you could touch it.

Taking it seriously in Barcelona

When we arrived at the Olympics we still didn't know which one of us would be dropped from the team. There was a bit of bad feeling when David found himself on the substitutes' bench. I think David felt that Tim Grubb, who had been living in America for years, should have been dropped even though Tim's horse Denizen was in very good form. But David had hurt his back and wasn't really one 100 per cent. I am sure that was the reason Ronnie left him out of the team.

In the Olympic Village I shared a room with John and Michael, and Tim shared with Ronnie – they both snore for England so I doubt they kept each other awake. The dressage riders and the event riders were in our apartment as well; we were all jammed in together.

Barcelona wasn't the crack that Seoul had been and it was more humid as well. There was no air conditioning and Spain in August can be very hot. The jumping was held at the Club de Polo where the Barcelona Show is usually held. The lovely grass arena was ripped up and replaced with sand and a new stabling complex was built.

The horses travelled out on Chris Goosen's lorry; he came along as our entertainments manager, driving us from Royan to Barcelona. We didn't participate as much at Barcelona as we had at Seoul. We didn't make it to the opening or closing ceremonies but we managed to go and support the Eventers out on the golf course in the mountains. We enjoyed ourselves but we were taking the job seriously. With Milton, Monsanta, Dollar Girl and Denizen we had four of the world's top horses. We thought we had a strong team; this was going to be our Games.

Throughout my jumping career, I was always first to go for the team. Ronnie says he put me there because I was organised and he knew I would be ready on time. The Team competition had an early start, eight in the morning. I remember walking the course. It was pretty big but I wasn't worried because Dollar Girl was on good form.

Starting off on the course she was jumping fantastic, she never put a toe on a pole but it was a very long course, sixteen jumping efforts. She was jumping so well, putting in such a lot of effort, that when I turned away from the entrance towards the final fence I think she just decided that she'd done enough. In retrospect, I don't think it was really anything to do with the water, although it was a big, full-size water jump with two spooky curly planks over it. The sun hadn't really got up, the ring was very bright in one part and in the shade it was very dark; it threw a bad light on the water.

That was the excuse everyone makes for her, but I am sure she just thought, 'Sod it – I've put in so much effort, do I really have to turn away from the entrance and keep going?' Sure enough, when she got to the water she stuck her head down and said, 'No'. We were clear until then, the last fence. I turned her away and tried again but she dug her toes in three times and was eliminated. I couldn't believe it. For a horse that had been jumping so well to be eliminated, it was odd.

I really felt for the other team members because it put them under intense pressure. I had been eliminated, they were now a team of three, there was no discard score available. When they went in the ring they knew their round would have to count. I know if is a little word with a big meaning but if I had have gone clear in that round I think it would have built up the lads' confidence.

I went out and got off. I didn't bother to school Dollar Girl or build a fence outside which was like the water, I just left her alone with Mark. I felt as sick as a Blackpool donkey. In the second round, she jumped the water with no problem but had two down. The Olympics were over for me.

In the Individual competition I ended up biting the dust at the triple bar. Tim Grubb and Denizen also bit the dust; then John and Milton had an unlucky peck in the double of oxers and had to pull out of the second part, having jumped in too big. And Monsanta gave up going down the combination. The combination was big: vertical, oxer, oxer. Monsanta knew he couldn't make the back rail so he simply jumped the front rail, diving down between the front and back rails. Nothing dangerous, the horse just knew he couldn't make the spread. It was quite smart of him really.

It wasn't our year. All in all, it was a miserable Olympics.

Back at the yard

After I returned from Barcelona, I was still in shock that I had been eliminated. Apollo had been rested after the Seoul Olympics, but that wasn't going to happen to Dollar Girl. After all, she'd hardly done anything and the journey to Spain was not arduous. I went to Rotterdam where we finished sixth in the Grand Prix. No repeat of the refusal, it was just as I thought, a one-off. But Dollar Girl didn't really seem to be enjoying her jumping.

I jumped her indoors throughout the rest of the year without winning much so after Berlin in December I decided to give her a complete break to see if I could freshen her up, much to Joe Haller's disgust. He couldn't understand why a horse had to be rested for four months in the field. He really was one of those owners who thought horses were money machines, not animals.

The way in which I had prepared her for the Barcelona Olympics was not how I would normally operate. I would not have rushed around trying to get as much mileage on the clock as possible. But I had had to because I only had a couple of months to get used to her. I decided to put her in the field and start afresh next year.

It proved to be the right decision because '93 was a good year for Dollar Girl. 1993 and onwards were the best years of her life. She won a good class in Rome, the Grand Prix in St Gallen, Ascona and Calgary where the Du Maurier was worth $250,000. It was my second win in that prestigious event.

She then went on and jumped indoors all that winter, winning consistently. Throughout her career Dollar Girl won over a million pounds.

She was by Dynamo, 16.1 hands, Hanovarian. She was very kind and could be ridden by almost anybody, which is why I taught Kevin Mahoney how to ride on her. The most expensive riding-school horse ever! And she was very popular with the grooms. If ever there was a horse with human qualities, it was Dollar Girl.

It was essential to keep the balance of her foot correct in order to keep her sound. She wasn't the soundest horse in the world, she had very delicate feet. I once sent her down to David Nicholson's at Jackdaw Castle because she was a bit lame on the turn, but sound on a straight line. She had to be kept fairly fit, so I asked David to have her so that her canter-work could be done on the perfect surface of his gallop. But I never thought to send her own feed with her and David was pumping high-protein racehorse feed into her; it wasn't doing wonders for her blood.

When I got her back she was sound and fit, but incredibly fresh.

I took her to Rotterdam where she tied up very badly with azoturia and we had to put her in a trailer to take her back to the stables. It took a week or ten days to get her blood right; she was suffering from protein poisoning.

Towards the end of the year, Julie Leonard, know to her friends as Cilla, left Paul Schockemohle and came to work for me. Cilla had driven all over Germany for Schockemohle and had an HGV driving license – when the horses went to a show with Mark Beever I had had to employ a driver for the horsebox which needed to be HGV in order to accommodate six horses. So Cilla was a god-send as she could drive and groom. Two for the price of one! I had met Cilla a few years earlier when she worked for Sue and Freddie Welch and she came highly recommended.

A horsebox needs to be an HGV in order to have enough space for six horses and living accommodation but Mark Beever didn't have an HGV drivers licence so whenever the horses went to a show I had to employ a driver to go with him. Towards the end of the year, Julie Leonard, a.k.a. Cilla, left Paul Schockemohle and came to work for me. She already had her HGV drivers licence and since arriving she has driven the horsebox and groomed at international shows all over Europe. I had met Cilla a few years earlier when she worked for Freddie Welch and I knew she could be relied on to take care of my horses and she had driven all over Germany for Schockemohle so I felt confident she could handle a large horsebox. Show jumpers are very valuable, so a careful driver is essential.

CHAPTER TWENTY THREE

The Racing Bug Bites

Liaising with the Duke – David Nicholson – about Dollar Girl gave me the racing bug again. It had never really gone away.

I told David I fancied having a couple of Point-to-Pointers that I could train myself and he suggested I called David Minton who used to work for the British Bloodstock Agency. Through David I bought Jolly Roger, who had run under rules and had a bit of form, together with a young horse called Mystic Mickey, a five-year-old. My brother Michael was riding Point-to-Point and I set about getting my new horses fit. A lad called Tony Brown, who had previously worked for Martin Pipe, was based with me and I decided he was the best person to look after the pointers. Tony took a real interest in them, instigating a fitness regime and taking charge of their feeding. Basically he took over looking after them.

At first we worked them around a field in the village owned by the late John Deaner. It had a steep hill, perfect for canter work. Then in the winter it became too wet so we took them over to the nearby gallop of trainer Annabel King at Wilmcote. Annabel is married to Irishman Aiden Murphy. This was to prove to be the start of a long and successful partnership between Aiden and me. Aiden is probably one of the most successful bloodstock dealers in this country and has a real eye for a horse. We became good friends and drinking partners.

We had Jolly and Mickey ready to run at the first meeting of the season in January and on Christmas Eve I thought I would take them over to Jackdaws Castle to have a good blow out.

My brother Michael rode Jolly and I was on Mystic Mickey. Halfway up the long gallop he started to cough. I immediately pulled up, jumped off and within seconds the horse dropped down dead. He had burst an artery in his lung. I had been incredibly lucky because if I hadn't jumped off he could have trapped me underneath him when he fell to the ground. Back at the yard everyone was very upset but Mickey had an aneurism, it was no one's fault, it could not have been avoided.

Jolly Roger turned out to be quite useful, having two seconds Point-to-Pointing and two seconds in Hunter Chases at Nottingham and Bangor, all with Michael riding him. Sadly, he then broke down in front at a Hunter Chase meeting at Cheltenham.

Many years before, I had been hunting in Ireland with Eddie Macken. We were out one day with the Meath and we needed to cross a river. We had to jump in, wade across and then jump out the other side. There was a plucky grey pony in front of me who leapt straight into the river, unseating his jockey. The pony clambered out the other side and I fished the little kid out. He was absolutely drenched, he must have been about ten I guess. I said, 'Get up mate, get back on, what's your name?' to which he replied, 'Adrian Maguire.'

At David's I met up with Adrian Maguire again. He reminded me that I had rescued him from the river in Ireland and we became firm friends.

A block of land came up for sale at the back of the farm; it ran from the edge of my land to the motorway and the price was right. I haggled with the agents and bought about 36 acres and built a sand gallop for the racehorses. It was on a curve and had a nice pull up the hill to give the horses something to work at. Sheep grazed the fields and would wander on to the sand, scattering as the horses cantered along. The show jumpers used it as well and I am sure it helped a lot with their fitness. Part of the land fronted the lane and there was a big barn and planning permission for a farm cottage. The whole deal had a lot of potential.

After the success with Jolly Roger I asked Aiden Murphy to find me another nice horse for hunter chasing and he found one for me in Cork. It had won two Point-to-Points, one by a distance. He was called Carrots and was owned by a dear old lady, Betty Sykes.

Carrots did actually win for me. He was second the first time out

Showtime jumping her heart out at the Atlanta Olympics

Left: Waiting to walk the course at Hickstead
Below: Bettina's daughter, Michelle

Above: Bettina and me at one of our charity balls
Below: Taking a nap at Aachen

Above: Jumping Arco at Hickstead in the 6-year old Championship. One horse I wish I was still riding
Below: Daniel at Hickstead on his pony Bodyguard

Above: Harry in full flight at Hickstead on his pony Welsh Wonder
Below: Mother on holiday in Spain

Above: My sister Sally propping up me and my brother Michael at one of our New Year's parties
Below: The look on my face says it all! It was even more uncomfortable than it looks. On holiday in Portugal, Pat Hales on the right

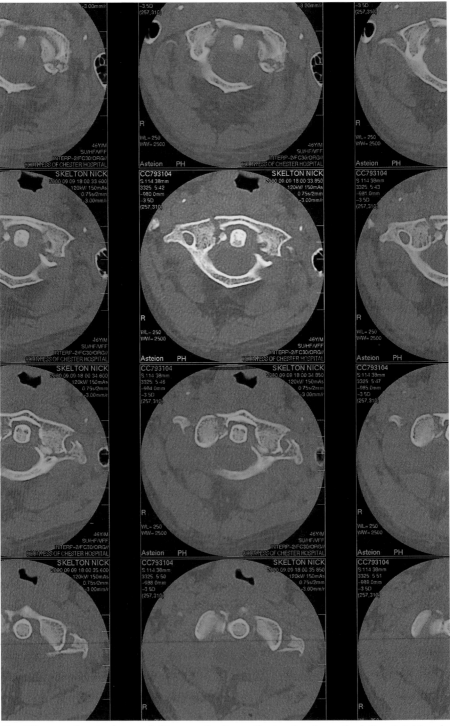

The C.T. scan of my broken neck. You can clearly see the two breaks on the left and right and the piece of bone floating on the end of the ligament

in a Point-to-Point and he won his second race for me, only to break down afterwards and never run again. He was retired and went to hack around the lanes with Martin Charles' girlfriend.

That was the end of my time as a trainer but I was still suffering badly from the racing bug. I told Aiden, 'Training these horses is a load of bollocks, they keep breaking down.' He listened sympathetically. I went on, 'If you see a nice mare by Strong Gale, I'd like one.'

Just that. 'A nice mare by Strong Gale. I'd like one.' Aiden is amazing at finding horses. He scouted around and found Certainly Strong for me. She had never run and I sent her to David Nicholson to train. This was serious stuff. Certainly Strong won her first race, a bumper at Ludlow and was second the second time out at Uttoxeter, again a National Hunt flat race. David's claimer, Robert Massey rode her in those races.

Adrian Maguire took over the ride on Certainly Strong and she ran her first race over hurdles at Haydock Park and won. It was Adrian's 500th winner and David's 1,000th winner. She was now moving into the bigger leagues and went on to win again and be placed second over hurdles. In her novice chasing year she won two Grade One Novice Chases. Every time out, she was always first or second. The show jumpers were having a lean time of it that winter and Certainly Strong really did help to keep the yard going with her winnings. After Adrian was injured in a fall, Richard Dunwoody rode her. They were both friends of mine and I always like her to be ridden by one of them.

With Richard Dunwoody, Certainly Strong won her second Grade One Novice Chase and he kept the ride on her until Adrian was back in the saddle. At the end of the season at Newbury in the Mares Novice Hurdle Final she was sixth.

Part way through the season, Certainly Strong didn't have a race lined up for a few weeks so I asked if she could come home for a break and go in the paddock. The Duke wasn't very happy about it but he finally agreed. I sent Mark down to fetch her in the horsebox and Certainly Strong came back with enough feed to last her through the break and exact, detailed instructions from David on how she was to be exercised!

The next season she went Novice Chasing. She was doing well that year and was one of the favourites for the Arkle Novice Chase at the Cheltenham Festival. But misfortune struck and two weeks before the race she sustained a hairline fracture of her pedal bone. She couldn't run, she was finished for that year. The bone was operated on and two screws inserted into the pedal bone. She healed up and came out strongly the following season to win another Handicap Chase.

In the meantime, Aiden Murphy found another good unraced, unnamed youngster by Strong Gale. We bought it jointly, half shares each, and we had a bit of fun naming it. We didn't know what to call it and came up with some ridiculous ideas. Then we had a brainwave. Whenever David Nicholson wanted to call to his wife Dinah he always shouted, 'Oi, mother!', pointing his index finger at her. We decided this was a great name and it stuck. The horse raced as Oi Mother. It won a bumper and a novice hurdle before being sold to an American for breeding, together with Certainly Strong.

Adrian Maguire was often injured in falls. The time he broke his arm, I took him off to a show, Jerez, in the south of Spain. We were down there with Malcolm Pyrah, Peter Murphy and a few other riders. One night we went out and found an Irish Bar. Straight away, Adrian was at home. We were in the bar, on the Guinness and Adrian – being a jockey and therefore quite slight – didn't take as much filling up as we did. At the end of the night, Peter Murphy and I literally carried him for about a mile back to the hotel. Adrian was sharing a room with me and we had great difficulty easing him through the doorway, comatose, horizontal and with a broken arm.

Malcolm's room was just across the corridor, and at breakfast the next morning he asked us, 'Did you two steal a piano last night?' We were flummoxed. 'No,' we replied. 'Well,' said Malcolm, 'all I could hear was, 'left a bit, right a bit' ... it sounded like you two were trying to get a piano into the room!' That was no piano we explained, just the wounded Maguire.

Another time when Adrian was grounded he and his girlfriend Sabrina came on holiday to Bermuda with Bettina and me. Like Richard Dunwoody, Adrian became bored when he couldn't ride.

We were the guests of Robert and Rosemary Ockendon-Day, whose daughter Rebecca had trained with me for a season and bought a good horse called Corrizienne.

Robert and Rosemary used to live in Bermuda and they had some friends there called the Haycocks. They let us have the use of their pool house, in the grounds of the main house. It was tremendous fun. We hired mopeds and drove around the island, two of us on each moped. The girls were very trusting I must admit!

Later on. Adrian married Sabrina and they had a baby, Shannon. Their wedding in Killarney was a party not to be missed. I had to take a flight the next day to Calgary. I woke up in Killarney, got on a plane and the next thing I knew I was waking up in Calgary. I am godfather to their second child, Finny.

On the Wednesday evening during the Cheltenham Festival, David Nicholson always had a party. Aiden Murphy and I had been racing and then stopped off at The Plough in Ford on the way back to Jackdaws Castle. We didn't get to David's until eight or nine o'clock that evening by which time Aiden was totally out of his tree. We went in and sat down at the table in the dining room with David, Dinah, David Minton, a few others and HRH The Princess Royal. The next thing there was a thump and I looked round only to discover that Aiden had fallen straight off his chair on to the floor. Princess Anne looked round and commented dryly, 'It looks like Aiden's enjoyed himself today!'

In August 1994 Bettina finally moved in with me. Since Sarah had left, Bettina had been shuttling to and fro between her own home in Germany and my home in England, but now she felt the time was right for her to settle down and bring her ten-year-old daughter Michelle to live at Sandall House Farm. Michelle was installed at Wroxall Abbey School where she started to learn English. Although a bit shy for the first year or so, Michelle has developed into a confident young lady and speaks impeccable English.

Bettina set about redecorating the house and putting her own style on the place. For over three years a woman's touch had been missing and there was a lot to be done. She is an excellent cook and I was very happy to be looked after properly again! I had been relying on takeaways for too long.

CHAPTER TWENTY FOUR
I Had a Dream

The 1995 Volvo World Cup Final was memorable for the kerfuffle over the television rights. The final was held in Gothenburg, where the headquarters of the sponsors, Volvo, were based. The FEI had made a cock-up by selling sole TV rights to the final to DSF, a German TV company, and Volvo were poised to pull out of the sponsorship. Winning a top-of-the-range Volvo car is one of the highlights of the World Cup and losing Volvo would have been a big blow to the sport. When Volvo finally pulled out in 1998, after twenty years, they had helped to establish the World Cup as one of the most prestigious events on the show jumping calendar.

Throughout the 1994/95 winter season Dollar Girl had qualified for the final at a variety of shows: Mill Street, 's-Hertogenbosch, all over. Even though riders are allowed to compete with two horses in the final, I only took Dollar Girl to Gothenburg. She had benefited from her racehorse training and was very fit and strong. She would need to be. Without a stable companion to share the load, the World Cup is a tough competition.

Having only one horse at the final I was able to focus completely on Dollar Girl and we got off to a fairly good start on the first day, finishing fifth in the speed leg – a Table C competition over a more-or-less Table A course. Eddie Macken won with Miss FAN, a horse he had only been riding for two months. On the second day we were seventh. Michael Whitaker and Two Step came in third but were leading overall, with Dollar Girl and me just three faults behind. Franke Sloothaak was half a fault behind in third place. Eddie and Miss FAN disappeared down the ratings to fifteenth.

165

I am sure that having only Dollar Girl to focus on helped me. I worked her every day and then on the day off I wandered over to the show but didn't work her. Dollar Girl rested and slept most of the day. I went to bed early that night as well. A first for me.

I had a dream that night, and woke up on the Sunday morning telling Bettina, 'I'm going to win this final.'

I went down to the stables to work Dollar Girl. Less than one fence covered the top three placings and there was a bunch of other good combinations just behind us. In the first of the final two rounds, Michael and Two Step picked up twelve faults to drop them well down the grid. I made a mistake at the first part of the second last and Franke with Weihaiwej had a single fence down as well. But Lars Neiberg and For Pleasure went clear to take the lead.

I was starting to feel less psychic. Maybe it had been just a dream, not a vision.

Going into the second round Lars was leading on five faults and I was lying second with seven. We were jumping in reverse order and I was able to put pressure on Lars by going clear. Dollar Girl jumped her heart out. There was a triple bar two from the end and she turned herself inside out to clear it. She really tried for me.

When Lars went into the ring I couldn't bear to watch. For Pleasure was jumping fantastic and when he cleared the huge triple bar I thought it was all over. But Lars had had to push hard for the triple bar and he couldn't get the nine-year old stallion back for the next fence. He brought it down to finish on nine faults, leaving Dollar Girl the winner. I was ecstatic. Ten years earlier I had been the understudy with St James, I knew how Lars felt, but Dollar Girl had been brilliant. She deserved to win.

Lesley McNaught, my team-mate from the old days at Edgars, had determinedly worked her way up the pack to finish third with Doenhoff.

By the time I arrived home in Warwickshire, a raucous party was already going in the Durham Ox, my local pub. Tracey, wife of the landlord Terry Liggins, was notorious in the area for taking her top off behind the bar. She could really draw a crowd and was on top form that night.

Buying and selling

Back in 1995 I had quite a few young horses and I needed a stable jockey to bring them on and take them to local shows. Alison Bradley had been on the team with me when we won a Silver Medal at the European Championships at St Gallen and I asked her if she would like to be based at Sandall House Farm, along with her horses. She liked the idea and along with her groom, Debbie Brooks, Alison came to live in Warwickshire, bringing her horses, Endeavour and Tinka's Boy, both owned by Mr and Mrs Sibcey.

One day at the Aldershot Show, Mr and Mrs Sibcey suddenly told me that they wanted to sell both of Alison's horses. This was a disaster for a young rider like Alison, but it happens, it is just part of show jumping. Bettina had always liked Tinka's Boy and she bought him. Endeavour was sold to American rider Debbie Dolan.

Alison is still bringing on young horses, and now lives with my brother Michael; they have a son called Charlie who is my youngest nephew. My sister, Sally, has a son Nicholas, who was born back in 1990. We have all had sons, we don't have a daughter between the three of us!

Tinka's Boy was only six when we bought him and I started riding him in '97. He took part in his first Nations Cup in La Baule and then competed in Gijón where Swiss rider Marcus Fuchs expressed interest on behalf of one of his owners. Basically, we were made an offer we couldn't refuse and sadly he was sold.

I thought a lot of Tinka's Boy, he was always destined for the top and he has proved me right with Marcus Fuchs. He is probably the best horse in the world at this present time. He was easy to ride, not at all complicated, he had a great mind. I have bred three foals by him out of Florida, the good mare I swapped with John Whitaker.

At about the same time, I had been sent a horse called Zalza from Joop Aaldering, a Dutch horse dealer whose wife Kyra had been riding him. Zalza was a very talented, pretty little chesnut horse but he could be quite difficult. Bettina really liked him and she bought him for me to ride. He won a couple of Grand Prix and the Masters at Olympia before being sold to Robert Smith. The horse is now in America.

Sally, my sister, had a friend who had been paralysed in a swimming accident. The lad really needed an electric wheelchair, but they are very expensive, and Sally hit upon the idea of holding a horse show to raise the funds to buy the wheelchair. She enlisted my help, my fields and most of my staff!

Sally had never run a horse show before, but like a Sergeant Major she set to work, drafting in Jackie Hobday and Gaye Williams to help her. Not content with helping to run the show, Jackie and Gaye organised a Ball at the same time, raising funds for the British Equestrian Olympic Fund and the BSJA. A huge marquee was erected, dance floor installed, lighting, the lot. We held the Balls for years and had some tremendous fun. In the autumn we would host the Injured Jockeys Fund Ball, held the night before the Hatton Team Chase.

The show ran successfully for two years before it grew so large that we needed more land. A good friend of mine, Melvyn Barraclough agreed to let us use his land at Arden Park Farm for the next three years. Melvyn trains a few racehorses and he's a lovely man. He'd do anything for me, I don't know anyone who would say a bad word about him.

I lose my favourite horse

Whenever Daniel and Harry were staying with me, every morning, first thing, they would run down to the yard and give Oxo his feed. One day we were all up especially early to go to the New Forest Show and they were down at Oxo's stable before the grooms were up. They found Oxo lying dead in his stable. He had died in his sleep. It was a nice way for him to go, but the boys were very upset.

I rang my dad to tell him and he arranged for Carey Sage to bring a JCB over and bury Oxo next to my old dog Dora in the field.

It was a pretty dismal day at the show, but we arrived home to a story that lightened the atmosphere. By the time Carey arrived with the JCB to dig the hole it was raining. My dad was directing operations from underneath his umbrella. As Carey lowered Oxo into the hole, my dad stepped back and the metal of the umbrella touched the electric fence – it's a mains electric fence, not battery operated, and he got an awful shock and nearly fell in the hole with Oxo.

And then I lose my second favourite horse

The following year at the final in Geneva, Hugo Simon and ET beat Willie Melliger and Calvaro in the jump-off for first place, leaving Dollar Girl just one fault behind in third place. 1996 was proving to be a good year for her despite her being sixteen years old. I had no plans to retire her, I felt she still had plenty of life in her and she was really enjoying her jumping.

At the beginning of December I smelt a rat when Joe Haller rang up and asked me to bring a cheque for his share of Dollar Girl's prize money to Olympia. Previously he had never done this, I usually took his cheque to Zurich in the spring. That's when I always saw him, after my annual audit.

I told Bettina that I thought it was a bit odd that Joe Haller wanted his prize money early, it just didn't feel right. I took the cheque to Olympia and gave it to him on the first day, which was a mistake.

Dollar Girl was sixth on the first day and then I rode her in the World Cup qualifier where she finished fifth. I had an unlucky fence down but the time was quite quick. As I came out of the ring, Joe Haller was standing there and he looked up and said to me, 'That's the last time you'll be riding her, she's going to Mexico to be retired.'

I couldn't believe my ears. I was gobsmacked. It was the first I had heard of it. My immediate thought was that Mexico was a long way to go to be retired. Joe had previously agreed that when she retired she would stay with me in England and we would try and breed from her. I wanted her to finish her days with me, bearing in mind that she was the pet of the yard and everyone adored her.

I asked him where she was going and he replied, 'I've given her to Alfonso Romo.' I distinctly remember him saying he had given her to him. Joe Haller went on to tell me that Alfonso Romo had agreed to let him have the first foal from her and that Jan Tops would take Dollar Girl home from Olympia with him.

I immediately went to find Jan and ask him what the hell was going on and he denied knowing anything about it. But I was having none of it. I insisted, 'Come on Jan, you know everything Alfonso Romo is doing, you might as well tell me the truth.' Whereupon Jan replied, 'Mr Romo paid for her last week at the show in Geneva.' Clearly Joe was lying, he had not given Dollar Girl to Alfonso Romo, he had sold her. I was appalled. How could someone sell a horse into retirement after all she had done for him over the years?

Joe Haller wasn't anywhere to be found, I didn't see him for a day or two, I thought maybe he had gone home. But he hadn't. The next time I clapped eyes on him he was outside the Royal Box upstairs at Olympia. I confronted him and told him exactly what I thought of him. At one point, I nearly had my finger down his throat, I was shaking my finger at him, so close to his face. Ann Martin, who writes for Horse and Hound and the Evening Standard was there, trying to get the story from him.

She certainly got a good story. I remember telling him the only good thing that would come out of it would be that I wouldn't have to see his fucking face around the shows any more.

It really was getting quite heated and then Haller just walked away. As he left, a policeman who was on duty outside the Royal Box came up to me and asked if I had a problem. I told him 'Yes, that's the bastard that's just sold my horse from underneath me.' To which the policeman replied, 'You should have hit him then!'

On the last night of Olympia, the organisers held an impromptu retirement ceremony for Dollar Girl. I jumped a fence and then took her saddle off. She got a standing ovation while the commentator outlined her glittering career, telling the crowd how much she had won. I swear Dollar Girl knew something was going on. All throughout Sunday she wouldn't eat, she was restless. She knew something was wrong and she really had the sulks on. All the children, Daniel, Harry, Michelle, the grooms, we all went to her stable to say our last goodbye to her. She knew she was going.

Of all the horses I have had, and I've been lucky enough to have some very good horses, I think Dollar Girl had everything. She had character, manners, ability – she must have been well behaved because she was the only horse Bettina ever liked to ride!

Dollar Girl now lives in Monterrey in Mexico and has had several foals. Every now and then we hear from someone who has seen her and they tell us she seems happy enough.

CHAPTER TWENTY FIVE

Who Wants to be a Millionaire

Back in the mid-Nineties I was riding a horse of Sue Welch's called Sublime, we had bought her out in California from Larry and Hilary Mayfield. One day Freddie Welch rang me to tell me he had come across two Australian women who were looking to buy a couple of top horses and that he would like to bring them to have a look at Sublime.

The two Australians, Evelyn Burton and Leila Andre, were in London looking for domestic staff and they had contacted Frances Hutchinson who runs a staff agency. Frances also owns Arabs and Show Hunters so when Burton and Andre expressed an interest in buying a show jumper, she introduced them to a good friend of hers, Marjorie Ramsay, who in turn introduced them to Sue and Freddie Welch.

The Australians wanted to get into horse sport in a big way. They were real high rollers and lived a very wealthy lifestyle. Evelyn Burton arrived at my yard in a chauffeured Bentley, Freddie was in his own car. I showed her Sublime and she then asked if I had anything else. I thought she might as well take a look at Tinka's Boy, after all, if she was interested in buying a horse for me to ride, then that is the horse I would really like to keep. She liked the look of Tinka's Boy and agreed to buy him and Sublime.

As we walked back towards the house, Burton took me to one side and quietly told me that she was looking to contract a rider to ride for her through to the Sydney Olympics in 2000. She would be willing to give them a good contract to ride her horses for five years. I asked her what sort of money she was thinking of paying. 'A million pounds a year for five years,' she replied. Well, it didn't take me long to agree that I would do it.

We had a cup of tea in the house and then she kept us entertained for about an hour talking about all the different things she had done in the world. She told us she was an investment banker and that she could double an investor's money in a short period of time. She wasn't very discreet and went on to tell us how much she was earning and how much money she was worth. I'm not much into investment banking and it all went whoosh, straight over my head.

On leaving, she invited me down to London for tea the following week at her hotel in Maida Vale. I arrived there to be met by the doorman. I asked for Miss Burton and he took me up to the top floor where she had the whole top floor, the penthouse. The butler took me into the drawing room where Evelyn was waiting for me. There was a silver tea service, the works. I sat down and she produced a contract, which we both signed; a million pounds a year for five years to ride her horses. Burton told me the money would be deposited in my bank account the following week during Olympia.

All the time, she talked about what she wanted to do for horse sport. She planned to sponsor Olympia the following year and Simon Brooks Ward gave her a hospitality box at the show. At Olympia I won the Masters with Zalza and when I went back up to her box after the class, Burton told me she liked the look of Zalza, how much would he cost? I named a price and she agreed to buy him as well as the other two.

What Burton maintained she would do for the horse sport in this country was nobody's business. She also offered to buy a horse for a girl called Lisa Murphy and would back her financially with horses and lorries. Two horseboxes were ordered from Oakley's, one for Lisa and one for me. At this point, Bettina and I thought we had died and gone to heaven, it was too good to be true.

By now, word was getting round that Evelyn Burton was a big spender and that things were going to happen. I kept asking her when I would receive payment for the horses and she kept telling me it was on its way. She then moved from the hotel in Maida Vale to Knightsbridge and invited us to dinner. We were met at the front door by a butler and then we all went to Scotts Restaurant for dinner. She had her whole family with her: mother, sister, auntie, granny, everybody was there. As time wore on, it became apparent that Evelyn Burton and Leila Andre were more than just good friends; they were lovers.

During dinner she told us she was buying the prestigious Hundridge Stud in Newmarket. There seemed to be no limit to her spending. Part way through the evening, a bloke walked in carrying a brown envelope and gave it her. She opened it in front of us all and produced a big wad of £50 notes. You could have choked a donkey with it, and she proceeded to shove it down her bra.

Every time I asked Burton when I would receive payment for the horses she stalled; the money was on its way, the money was held up in China, then in Russia, then in Hong Kong. That money was held up in practically every country in the world. She sponsored an Arab Show at Haydock Park and agreed vast prize money, which had never been heard of before in Arab showing classes, but no one ever received their prize money. One day she turned up at Windsor and promised to sponsor Windsor the following year. Simon Brooks Ward arranged for her to have a hospitality table but she never paid for it and she was invited to sit in the Royal Box.

Burton and her girlfriend Leila Andre then moved in with Frances Hutchinson's mother Nadia. They were invited to stay for a weekend and ended up staying sixteen weeks. It seems they treated the house like it was a hotel, insisting the heating be kept on maximum and making endless telephone calls.

Then Burton and Andre moved into a hotel in Hertfordshire. They took the whole of one floor but didn't pay, they just made a lot of promises. Eventually, the owner of the hotel got fed up with them not paying their bill so one day he sounded the fire alarms, evacuated the place, double locked their doors so they couldn't get in and called the police.

Evelyn Burton's cover was blown when she signed a contract to buy the Hundridge Stud. It was, of course, a legally binding contract and the selling agent, Ian Blatchley, took her to court for the money to pay for the Stud when she didn't come up with the funds on completion date.

Burton was investigated for fraud and subsequently sent to jail for five years, along with her lover, Leila Andre, who was sent down for three years. All the time they had been in England they had been conning money out of wealthy, sophisticated people by offering to invest it, promising to 'double your money' and then spending it on their own hedonistic lifestyle instead.

During the investigation it came to light that they owned and ran a brothel in Melbourne called Magic Moments. Leila's leather-clad alias was 'Madame Xavier'!

CHAPTER TWENTY SIX
It's Showtime in Atlanta

Sue Welch's mare Showtime was eleven years old. She was in the prime of her life and began the Olympic year by winning the Grand Prix in Madrid, then taking second place at both Lisbon and Barcelona. For three consecutive weeks, she had top places at major shows and Showtime was selected for the British team to go to Atlanta.

Tim Grubb had taken US nationality and was now riding for the Americans, leaving the fourth slot in the team vacant. John Whitaker was selected with Keeley Durham's Welham, Michael Whitaker was taking Two Step, I had Showtime and the new recruit was Geoff Billington and It's Otto. Robert Smith and Tees Hanauer were non-travelling reserves. Arrangements were made so that they could be flown out as late as 25 July if they were needed. Malcolm Pyrah came with us as team trainer.

The horses were flown out to Atlanta three weeks before the competition so they could acclimatise to the hot, humid, Georgia weather. Show jumpers are used to arriving at a show and then competing, almost immediately. The horses were all jumping well in training but they were there for such a long time that psychologically it must have been a strain for them. After all, they don't know the schedule, they never really know which is the day you will be asking them to perform their best. The horses went for weeks, wondering when the show would be.

As far as we lads were concerned we were all going to be together for a long time, and at times like that you need to be with a good team, otherwise boredom sets in. We were used to being very busy all day and to suddenly be dropped in a strange place and only have one horse to ride was alien to us. We riders had a lot of time on our hands and nothing to do. We went to watch the eventing, we walked their course, but it was generally pretty boring. Atlanta isn't exactly the biggest tourist trap in the world and we were loose-endish. We stayed in the Village for the first couple of weeks but we wanted to be closer to the horse park during the competitions so then we moved out to the White Columns Inn, owned by Epp Wilson, Master of the Belle Meade Hunt. Epp's father, James Wilson, owns Pine Top Farm, the USET (United States Equestrian Team) Combined Training Center, so he was quite used to the foibles of horsey folk.

The facilities were good in the Village. Ronnie and Malcolm shared a room, Michael was with Geoff and John bunked down with me. We had our own apartment in Atlanta, it wasn't like Barcelona where we were crammed in with the eventers and dressage riders. Team vet Marc Suls shared the apartment with us as well.

After a while, the boredom developed into a routine. Every evening we used to go to a laptop bar. We assumed it would be a sort of cyber café, but it wasn't. We never spotted a laptop computer, but we spotted a few fast bits of work. The place was called Cheetah's but we spent so much time in there that we renamed it the Office.

One night we were coming back from the Office quite late, about eleven o'clock and somehow Ronnie and I got split up from the others. We wandered into the Village through the nearest entrance, which was actually the furthest point from our apartment, about a mile's walk away. Michael, John, Geoff and Malcolm went in through a different gate.

Ronnie didn't fancy walking all the way across the Village, quite frankly he didn't look like he was going to handle the walk. The normal bus service had wound down for the evening – instead of running every five minutes, it was now once an hour, it was late in the evening, there was nobody about.

If you've ever been to Disney World you will have seen the bus service they have there – a little tractor engine with half a dozen carriages, like a train. We went in through the gate and saw one of these little bus trains parked up nearby. There was no one with it.

I turned to Ronnie. 'Hey,' I said, 'there's a bus here, I'll drive it and you get on the back.' The keys were in the ignition and the CB radio was switched on. I don't know where the driver was, he must have nipped to the loo. I started it and Ronnie sat in the far back corner, about 30 yards behind me.

I set off driving through the Village and I could hear a guy calling out on the CB radio: 'Bus gone missing, bus gone missing, look out for the number 37, it's been stolen.'

I was trundling along back to our apartment when I drove around a corner and saw about fifteen or twenty athletes at the bus stop. I turned round and shouted back to Ronnie, 'What shall we do?' He said, 'Stop and pick them up.'

As I drove towards them, they surged forwards. I stopped and let them on. I set off again and around the next corner there was another bunch of athletes standing at the bus stop. By the time I was halfway to our apartment, my bus was full. Every now and then the CB radio would crackle into life: 'The number 37 bus has been stolen, look out for the number 37,' but I just ignored it. I thought it best not to reply. No one on the bus seemed worried, I guess they didn't understand English. Ronnie was still sitting in the far back right-hand corner and every time I turned around, he gave me the thumbs up. He was the conductor, he was in charge, as usual.

I pulled up at the food halls and luckily everybody got off, that's where they were all going. We drove on with another good half a mile to go and then just as we were nearing our apartment, as we were going down the hill past the Olympic pool, there were two black athletes standing at the bus stop. I pulled up and let them on and when we got to our stop I switched the engine off and got out. One of them said, 'Hey man, we wanna go to the restaurant,' to which I replied, 'Sorry mate, this is where my shift ends. You'll have to wait for the next driver.' God knows how long they waited before they realised no one was going to turn up. And the whole time the CB radio kept broadcasting, '37, has anybody seen the 37?'

Ronnie and I beat the other lads back to the apartment, we were sitting with our feet up watching television by the time they arrived.

Although we missed our usual fall guy, Broomie, we had a replacement – Geoff Billington. Every day we did something to Geoff. When you arrive at the Games, you are given lots of little gifts: hair shampoo, sunblock, aftershave, all sorts of things. One day, when Geoff was in the shower, John got hold of some haemorrhoid cream. We emptied Geoff's sunblock out of its tube and replaced it with haemorrhoid cream. Ronnie was clued up to what we were doing and when Geoff came out of the shower Ronnie said, 'Now lads, make sure you've got your sunblock on, because you'll get burnt today.' We all started putting sunblock on our faces, arms, legs, everywhere, and Geoff was plastering it all over his face, his arms, legs. We were having trouble keeping straight faces, Geoff was covered in haemorrhoid cream.

Next day, while Geoff was in the shower, we emptied all the haemorrhoid cream out and filled the tube with liquid shoe cream. Sure enough, on Ronnie's orders, we all smothered ourselves in sunblock and Geoff was plastered in shoe cream, all rubbed in, everywhere. Off we went, down to the stables.

The following day, we got caught out. It was Otto who gave the game away! John had emptied out the shoe cream and filled the tube with toothpaste. Again, Geoff plastered himself with it, face, legs, arms, everywhere. But when we arrived at the stables, Otto started licking Geoff. He said, 'There's something the matter with this horse, he keeps licking me. He's never done that before.' We all burst out laughing, whereupon Geoff smelt his arms and realised that he was all pepperminty. He knew something was wrong so we told him what we'd done. But he hadn't been sunburnt! You see, you don't need all that fancy expensive sunblock, shoe polish or haemorrhoid cream will do nicely.

Our performance in the Team Competition was startling in that we had gone to the Games as one of the favourites and we came out eleventh. The conditions had been appalling and the arena had flooded in the downpour but Showtime tried her hardest and jumped well to finish with eight faults and four; in the first round she put a foot in the water, which was unfortunate.

The whole team was castigated by the Press and some said we had taken the horses out there too early. But if we had taken them out later and they had suffered with the heat it would have been worse.

The fences for the Team Competition are built so that they don't bury the lesser nations who are sometimes riding horses who are not up to Olympic competition. But horses and riders have to qualify for the Individual, which allows the course builder to test the best. With hindsight, I should not have gone, even though Showtime had qualified. She had coped with the Team Competition, but the Individual was a different story.

It really was like driving a lorry in the red, she was always under pressure in the first round. She actually went round for four, which is good, although she went in the water again. But the second round was very big and difficult and she had had enough by then, she had come to the end of her tether. There was a double of walls and she took one look and ran at them. She just wanted to get it over and done with as quick as possible and get out of there. She had three down.

After Atlanta, Showtime continued to win consistently until she was retired in 2000. She was sixteen and went home to Sue and Freddie Welch's farm where she is in foal to Tinka's Boy.

CHAPTER TWENTY SEVEN
Virtual Village

Kevin Mahoney was no longer Managing Director at Everest, they were under new management and decided to move out of show jumping. The contracts with John, Michael and myself were obsolete and we lost our sponsorship.

We decided to stay together and try to attract a joint sponsor. John and Michael had always come as a package deal because they are brothers but we thought we would try to keep the three of us together.

John managed to come up with a sponsor for himself and Michael; Virtual Village, owned by David Heap. Sue Heap, David's wife, knew John many years ago in Yorkshire. He met up with her again at the Windsor Horse Show when she asked him if he had found a new sponsor. He hadn't and Sue offered, 'My husband will sponsor you.' But nobody realised that the person working as their stud manager was Greg Parsons, my old friend the chicken plucker from my days at Odnaull End Farm. Apparently, when David Heap told Greg that he was thinking of sponsoring John and Michael, Greg piped up, 'If you do that, you must sponsor Nick as well.' And very generously, they did.

Geoff Billington got wind of what we were up to and muscled in on the act. Virtual Village were now sponsoring the four of us and we were all decked out in their purple and yellow colours.

One evening, Sue and David Heap invited us all down to their house in Montpelier Square for dinner. Greg and Lottie Parsons were there, Sue and David, their daughter Annie, the two Whitakers, Geoff Billington and myself. It was quite a big party at the table. I was driving that evening. I had to get back to

Warwickshire that night, I couldn't stay over so I offered to drive. Consequently, I wasn't drinking.

It was just after Calgary and Michael's horse Touchdown, owned by James Kernan, had had colic out there and was left behind to be operated on. Michael was waiting for news, he wasn't happy, he was stressed and worried.

When we arrived the lads started drinking beer, then it was on to dinner and red wine. The evening was going well, everyone was getting well stuck into the wine and I was on water. We were trying to amuse and impress the Heaps with our stories, each trying to outdo the other. The lads had started out on their best behaviour, but it was starting to deteriorate. Michael kept making lewd offers to Sue Heap but she was fending him off nicely.

At about midnight Michael got a call from a fellow in the equine clinic in Canada. The line was poor and Michael thought the guy had said Touchdown was dead. Michael was devastated, he's very emotional at the best of times but the alcohol took over. He started crying. Michael said, 'I'm sorry about this, I just feel so sorry for James.' Next to me, John was crying as well, because he felt sorry for Michael. I thought, I don't believe this.

I'm reaching for my Perrier and they are on their twenty-fifth bottle of red wine. I glanced to the other end of the table and Sue and David Heap, and Annie, were all crying. I looked around the whole table. Everyone was in tears, they were all so upset that Touchdown was dead.

After a while everyone pulled themselves together and I said, 'Come on Geoff, it's about time we went home.' Geoff was dallying. I told him, 'If you're not there in two minutes, I'm leaving without you,' and went outside and got in the car. Geoff leapt in the car as I pulled away from the kerb and was asleep before we had gone a hundred yards.

The next day, I was on the tractor driving across the field when my phone rang. It was Geoff. 'Guess what?' he said. 'Touchdown's not dead at all.' All that weeping was for nothing. The Heaps must think we're a right lot.

Selling up

I like building. Planning, construction, change. I had built everything I could think of at Sandall House Farm: indoor stabling, outdoor stabling, indoor school, horse walker, winter stabling barns – you name it, I'd built it. I'd even tried to build a swimming pool in the garden of the house but the neighbours objected and I had to abandon the plan.

I had loads of stables but not many horses, the place took a lot of maintenance and maintenance just isn't as much fun as building. I decided I needed a new challenge so I put Sandall House Farm on the market. The land I had bought years earlier when I was training Pointers had planning permission for a farm cottage. I applied for permission to convert the barn into stabling and my idea was to move the horses and the staff to the new yard, just a field or two away, and to buy a completely separate house for Bettina, the children and myself.

As soon as I let it be known that Sandall House was for sale, Julia Tooth was on the phone to me. Julia and her husband Brian Smith, a good Irish rider, lived at Brook Furlong Farm, a short distance up the lane. They are now divorced but Brian was very obliging and used to ride a couple of horses for me.

Julia's father, Raymond Tooth, owned quite a number of useful thoroughbreds and she needed more space. They promptly made me an offer for Sandall House and sold Brook Furlong to Robert Smith. Julia now operates Raymond Tooth Racing who own Lear Spear, a good Group Two winner as well as a number of other useful flat horses.

Carey Sage had retired so I needed a new builder and Robin Hobday, aka Dobbin, came to my rescue. Along with his sidekick Dickie Dover, they built stables, a tack room, feed room and washroom inside the barn and I renamed the place Sanbrook Farm. The horses were moved into Sanbrook Farm, we moved out of Sandall House Farm and Bettina, Michelle and I found ourselves with nowhere to live. We rented a small cottage at Shrewley House up in the village and Julia let my grooms stay on at Sandall House until Dobbin had built the new farm cottage.

In the meantime, Bettina and I went house hunting. There was a large Victorian house in Rowington for sale that needed a lot of renovations. It seemed an ideal outlet for my creative building obsession and we moved into Finwood Lawn in November 1997. We have been renovating ever since and the place still isn't finished.

Finwood Lawn has a large staff flat on one side so the grooms were able to leave Julia's and come to live with me. All winter we waited for the farm cottage to be finished – it was April before they were able to move in.

The Duke Cannes can

Cannes is a lovely horse show, it's all very civilised there. Riders stay at the Majestic Hotel, right on the beach and the classes don't start until seven o'clock in the evening, allowing all day for sunbathing, lazing around the pool and recovering from the night before. In reality, the classes start so late because it is cooler for the horses, but it all makes for a good holiday. For obvious reasons, Bettina usually comes to Cannes with me, and that year we decided to take Aiden Murphy, his wife Annabel and David and Dinah Nicholson.

The Majestic offers specially reduced rates to riders, their families and friends – it is a lot less than the usual tariff. We all arrived, checked in and everyone went off to their own rooms. Bettina and I were unpacking when all of a sudden there was a knock at the door. It was the Duke. I opened the door and he had his finger out, pointing at me, and he said, 'Oi,' just like when he says 'Oi, mother,' but this time it wasn't mother, just 'Oi'.

'Oi,' he said again, 'I've told mother not to unpack 'cos I looked on the back of the bedroom door and the tariff is 11,000 francs a night.' The sterling equivalent is about a thousand pounds. The blood had drained from his face, 'We're not stopping here,' he finished.

'Don't worry,' I told him, 'it's all organised. The show rate is £100 a night.' The hotel reception had put him in a suite, but he was still only paying the bargain show rate!

Everyone enjoyed themselves and went to the show at night. There is a really good riders' hospitality box at Cannes; you get free drinks, champagne, food, everything. The Duke was having a great time and on the last night, as Aiden and I were chatting together, we could see him watching a performance by stunt rider Lorenzo, and as he watched he was quietly dancing away to the music, all on his own. He was well away.

Hopes are high

After moving house I started to think about retirement. I was only forty years old but I hadn't really got the horsepower any more. Showtime was in her twilight years, she was winding down and would soon call it a day. I felt that maybe I should call it a day, too.

I took Showtime on the Sunshine Tour to Barcelona, Lisbon and Madrid where she won the Grand Prix, proving she still had what it took. I was pleased. Sue and I both wanted her to go out at the top. But I was short of an up-and-coming top horse.

One day on the tour, I was chatting to Mike Bullman who was our Chef d'Equipe, bemoaning the fact that I really needed another top horse. Mike, who knows pretty much everything that's going on, mentioned that he had heard a whisper, that I would be offered a top horse. He told me, 'I think you're going to be getting Hopes are High.' He had heard it in passing, just in conversation, nothing definite.

I didn't really get my hopes up because Hopes are High was a nice horse and he was going well for his rider Andrew Davies, but he looked a bit difficult to ride. Andrew had jumped Hopes in the Nations Cup in Lisbon but it didn't look like an especially top horse at the time.

After I got home, David Broome called me. 'Hopes needs a stronger rider, I don't think Andrew will manage him at a bigger level,' he told me. I said, 'Yes, I'll try him, but what does Andrew think about this? Does he know about it?' I didn't want Andrew jocked off the horse without him knowing what was going on. It's happened to me and it's not very nice. Contrary to what Andrew's mother maintained at the time, I didn't call David and ask for the horse, it was offered to me.

Hopes are High arrived in time for the Royal Show at Stoneleigh, the same show in which I started out all those years back with Phoenix Park for David. I jumped in the big class on the all-weather surface. Hopes had the last fence down but felt very scopey. I could see what David meant when he said the horse needed a stronger rider. Sometimes Hopes trotted behind while still cantering in front. I call it cross-canter. He was actually quite difficult.

The following week we went to Hickstead for Royal International and jumped in the Kings Cup. It poured with rain and it was very deep ground. We were second, beaten by Robert Smith on Mighty Blue. From then on the horse improved in leaps and bounds. At the New Forest the next week he finished second in the Team Trials and third in the Daewoo Championship.

Next stop was Dublin. Hopes jumped a double clear in the Nations Cup and won the Kerrygold Grand Prix to take home £25,000. It was my fifth win at Dublin. The horse was starting to show some real form and David sold Hopes are High to Lord and Lady Harris, owners of a lot of good show jumpers and racehorses.

We had a short break and, now under new ownership, went to Gijón for a Nations Cup show. Hopes won the Grand Prix. By now, this was an unbelievable run of success. We came home, had a week off and Hopes flew out to Calgary along with Showtime. But in the Nations Cup at Spruce Meadows, the peg fell out, it all went wrong.

There was a line of fences down the centre of the ring and a related distance from the water jump to a set of curved planks. I jumped the water and tried to contain him but he started to trot behind. I don't know how many strides he had, or should have had, but he ended up with his head on the top of the planks, his knees on the floor and me on his ears. I pulled up. I thought it was a stop because he never actually reached the other side of the fence and I walked around thinking they would ring the bell and rebuild the fence.

Nothing was happening and I wasn't very happy. I walked

around and turned a few circles and then I threw my dolly out the pram and walked out of the ring, much to the horror of Ronnie. Technically, I was eliminated. They were now a team of three.

It seemed the judges thought that I had made a jump at the fence; they said I had left the floor and therefore should have carried on.

I telephoned Lord Harris to tell him what had happened; he always wanted me to call him whenever his horse jumped, he wanted to know what had happened, good or bad. He was a very keen follower of his horses. I told him that maybe I shouldn't bother going in the second round, perhaps Hopes should jump a few smaller classes, come home and regroup.

Lord Harris said that I might as well jump in the second round, it wouldn't do Hopes any harm. He installed a bit of confidence in me and we jumped round in the second for only four faults.

I walked the course for the Du Maurier the next day and it was big and difficult. That is nothing out of character for the Du Maurier, it is usually a very difficult course, after all you are jumping for $250,000!

There were only five or six clears and Hopes was one of them. We were last but one to go and the second course was huge. It was massive. And difficult. There were no clears before me and Hopes jumped clear but had half a time fault. I was happy with that. If the last horse jumped clear I would be second. It would be a good result. The last horse was It's Otto with Geoff Billington. The Du Maurier is famous for being won with only one double clear and when I came out with half a time fault I rushed back in to watch Geoff. I think he hit the third fence, an oxer over a water ditch, Otto had it down behind. That was it. I was the winner with a clear and half a time fault. My third Du Maurier. John Whitaker is the only other rider to have won it three times, with Milton, Gammon and Grannusch.

For Hopes are High it was his third consecutive CSIO Grand Prix win. We came home from Calgary and went on to Rome in the October for the World Equestrian Games. We joined Geoff with It's Otto, John Whitaker on Heyman and Di Lampard with Abbevail Dream and came home with a Team Bronze Medal.

On our day off, Bettina and I went shopping and I bought a new suit. Bettina loves shopping in Rome. We had arranged to meet Malcolm and Judy Pyrah, Graham Sparks and Penny Banks at the Hassler Hotel at the top of the Spanish Steps. From the top floor you get a beautiful view across the whole of Rome, it is one of the best hotels in Rome. We met for lunch at one o'clock and at about six o'clock, after numerous bottles of red wine, we moved downstairs to the cocktail bar where we continued our late lunch with a few bottles of champagne. Graham Sparks asked me what I had got in my bag. 'I've been shopping,' I told him and pulled out my new suit.

Graham is a good few sizes bigger than me and he proceeded to take off his jacket and trousers, in the bar, and put on my suit. The trousers were way up at half-mast and the jacket sleeves were up around his elbows. Meanwhile, we had been joined by David Broome who commented on the unusual Italian tailoring. After another bottle of champagne Graham was finally persuaded to give me back my suit.

We moved on to the Dambruzzo Restaurant where our late lunch continued. I can't remember what time we finished, I did what I am famous for, I fell asleep at the table. When I've had enough, I've had enough. I just go to sleep. I could sleep on a washing line.

Our lunch lasted at least twelve hours. It was a great way to spend a day off in Rome. I highly recommend it.

Graham Sparks is a great crack. I once rode a horse called It's Twix for him at Newark and Notts County Show. He and Malcolm owned the horse jointly but Malcolm, who usually rode him, was away in La Baule. I won the class. One ride, one win! Sparky rang Malcolm and told him, 'I've found myself a decent jockey. One ride, one win.' Apparently Malcolm replied, 'I suppose it's taken me three years to make the horse and him one day to wreck it!'

Hopes ended the year at Olympia and finished third in the Grand Prix. From July through to December he had won a total of £230,000.

CHAPTER TWENTY EIGHT
"Don't Worry, They'll Be Back

1998 had started off dismally but with the advent of Hopes are High it had ended on a good note. For once, the good times got even better. My secretary turned out to be psychic and just before Christmas that year Daniel and Harry came back to live with me at the new house. They were proving to be a bit of a handful for Sarah. Boys will be boys, they needed a bit more discipline.

They brought all their ponies with them, chickens and all. Daniel joined Michelle at Princethorpe College near Rugby and Harry went to school at Arden Lawn in Henley.

Virtual Village were cutting down on their sponsorships, so I was told. They continued to sponsor John, Michael and Geoff and I went my own way. No more team colours.

Equiline came to the rescue and sent me jackets, caps, show jackets, shirts, ties, bandages, bandage wraps and saddle pads. Horseware of Ireland sent rugs, all embroidered with my name.

With Hopes are High I had a good chance of making the Team for the Europeans which were being held at Hickstead. The campaign started at Modena, Cannes and Aachen; Hopes hadn't hit top form but he was going well. At the Royal Internatoinal he won the King George V Gold Cup, beating Ludger Beerbaum. At Dublin he was third in the Grand Prix. But he wasn't really the same horse as he had been the year before, something was bothering him. He was more difficult, I felt something wasn't quite right. We went to Calgary and he definitely wasn't sparking there.

In the Europeans at Hickstead we finished fourth in the first leg, a speed competition. In the Nations Cup he was clear until the last two fences when he ran off with me down a line of fences on related distances and he ended up like he had in Calgary, he pulled up. As he stopped, I think he landed on the foot of one of the big, oak Derby Rails. He circled and jumped it and finished the course, and jumped in the second round, but when he came out for the trot up the next day, he was lame. Hopes was taken to the veterinary college where they scanned his hoof which showed he had a hairline fracture of the pedal bone. I think it had been bothering him for a long time and landing on the foot of the standard aggravated it.

Hopes went home to David Broome at Mount Ballan. In addition to the fracture he developed an infection in his foot which went up the hoof instead of coming out. He was off the road for the rest of 1999 and all of 2000. I'm happy to say he's now sound and jumping with David's son, Matthew.

With Hopes sidelined, Lord and Lady Harris bought another horse for me to ride from Joop Aaldering. Lalique was eight years old but she taken time out to have a couple of foals so she was quite inexperienced. I felt she had real potential.

And another four horses had turned up on the yard for me to ride. The Italian rider Guido Dominici had tragically died young from a brain tumour and one day I had a call from Gary Widdowson's brother-in-law, asking me if I was interested in taking over the ride on Guido's horses. He was friendly with the owner Arianna Gilardoni, who lived in the Italian part of Switzerland.

I was short of horses, so they were sent over. They had not been worked for a few months and it took a while to get them fit. I took them to a little indoor show at Solihull, just to give them a warm up. It was 27 October. The first horse I jumped was Frisco, the horse Guido had considered the best of the bunch. Frisco jumped the first fence, went on to the second, a small oxer, and picked up a stride too early. He jumped into the middle of it, turned a somersault and I hit the floor. I was in a lot of pain and realised I had broken something. I was airlifted to hospital where they diagnosed a broken collarbone. This isn't a very serious injury so I was hopeful of being back in the saddle before the end of the year. I competed at Olympia but it was obvious something was wrong. I couldn't hold the reins properly, I had no strength in my shoulder and the pain indicated a problem.

I went for more X-rays which showed that the original diagnosis had not been correct; the collarbone had been shattered, not just broken. No wonder I was in pain – I was laid up for another couple of months. But I intended to be competing again in February, in time for the Sunshine Tour in Spain.

By the time February arrived, two of Guido's horses were lame and had to be sent back to Italy to be retired. Another was sold, leaving me with the good black stallion, Jalisco, who was the leading national horse in this country in 2000. He was then sold to Mike Dawson for Scott Smith to ride.

Early in November, soon after I first injured my collarbone, Aiden and I made our regular trip to the Fairyhouse Foal Sales in Ireland where we bought five National Hunt foals. While we were there I met up with John and Pat Hales who were also buying foals. John was the owner of the racehorse One Man, and had just bought the last relative of One Man at Fairyhouse. He was in a genial mood; we shared a taxi to the airport and flew back to Birmingham together. Their daughter Lisa rides, and I had met John and Pat around the shows where I always spoke to them but nothing more than general conversation.

A couple of weeks later Lisa Hales called me: her mother had a young stallion, would I be interested in riding it? I certainly was interested, and immediately agreed. The six-year-old stallion, Magic Darco, arrived at Sanbrook Farm shortly afterwards, at the end of December. In view of the fact that I was laid up until February, it is fortunate that Andrew Saywell, who had worked for me some years before, had come to live at Sanbrook Farm and was renting a yard across the lane. He rode the horses while I was off and was a great help to me.

Over the winter, Joop Aaldering called to tell me he had seen a nice horse and I should go and look at it. I told David Broome about it and suggested we bought it for Lord Harris. David and I went to Hamburg to see the horse. It was lovely, only six years old. Excited, we came back but we couldn't persuade Lord Harris to buy it. He thought it was too young, he wanted an older horse.

I was back in the saddle early in the year and went off to ride Pat

Hales' Magic Darco and a few other horses at the Sunshine Tour at Vejer in southern Spain that starts the second week of February. I stayed out there the whole six weeks, unusual for me, I tend to fly back and forth as a rule, and the horse I had seen in Hamburg was constantly on my mind. I really wanted it, I had a good feeling about it. One day I was talking casually to Lisa Hales and told her I had seen a really good stallion but couldn't find anybody to buy it.

I showed Lisa the video of it and she said, 'Send it to my dad.'

Daniel and Harry were going home to go back to school after half term, so I sent the video home with them, telling them to send it on to John Hales. A couple of days later, Lisa found me and told me that her father wanted to go and see the horse in the video; he liked the look of it.

I flew home in the middle of the week, flew to Hamburg with John Hales and his vet, David Jagger, and tried the horse. John Hales liked it, David Jagger

vetted it and we brought it home.

I was really excited about this horse. His name was Arko. He reminded me so much of Tinka's Boy, he had the same sort of qualities. I was getting keen again, my enthusiasm was back. No retirement for me! I could see a good string of horses coming along, being built up from the early stages. I felt sure Arko could take top slot in a few years' time. In John Hales I had a really good new owner, he was keen to build up a team of horses. Along with Sue Welch as an owner, I felt I had prospects. Two good owners upon whom I could rely; I could get back to the top again.

Throughout 2000, Arko really progressed. He qualified for the Foxhunter, Grade C, and the Six- and Seven-year-old Finals at the Horse of the Year Show. What I remember most was John Hales' enthusiasm as he drove me the length and breadth of the country trying to qualify. Especially after a few hard nights!

Following on from Arko's success, John decided he wanted to buy another horse. I went shopping in Holland again with Joop Aaldering and saw a good young horse. John was thinking of buying it.

CHAPTER TWENTY NINE

One More Fall

Lord and Lady Harris's new mare, Lalique, was coming along well and showing some form. She was inexperienced when she came to me and competing at county Shows was perfect grounding for her, traveling alongside her stable companion, Arko. She hadn't been a problem to me all the time I had had her.

In September we went up to the Parkgate Show near Chester. The weather was sunny, the ground was good, we were having a nice day. I had jumped in one class and got a feel for the ring: it was uneven, a bit hilly; it was on a bank so it wasn't level, it had gradients in it.

I was jumping Lalique in the International Trial; I jumped a wall and then turned back on myself to a triple bar going uphill. I think it was fence six or seven. The triple bar was quite wide. She was clear till then but I placed her a bit too close and on take off I couldn't push or help her, I had to sit still. I wasn't worried, Lalique would usually go, she didn't have a stop in her.

She took off in front but obviously thought she couldn't make the back rail, so she stopped and put back down again. Her front feet were over the front rail, she was in the middle of the fence.

When she took off, I quite reasonably expected her to jump the fence so I had gone forward expecting her to leave the floor. As she stopped I went up her neck and she put her head down. My hands were trapped underneath me, on the top of her head. At one point I suppose I was only eighteen inches off the floor. If Lalique had kept her head down I would have slid off safely.

But she didn't. She ran backwards and threw her head up, catapulting me into the air. All I can remember is landing right on the top of my head, with my full body weight above me. I wasn't on the angle at all, I dropped vertically from about five feet. I hit the floor and heard a loud crack, literally inside my head. A lady standing nearby heard it as well. As my head hit the floor I just dropped to one side.

I ended up lying on my back, facing the sky, a few feet back from the fence. Whenever I fall the first thing I do is to try and get up. But I just couldn't move. I had this amazing pain in the back of my head. I lay there motionless.

By this time, a lot of people had dashed into the ring: John and Pat Hales, my son Daniel, Robert Smith, Peter Charles. I was really scared. I couldn't move my arms and my legs, they were completely numb. The First Aid team and the Show Doctor came to me. They kept telling me to lie still because I kept trying to move, but I couldn't move at all.

I was conscious the whole time and kept complaining about the pain in the back of my head. Then after a couple of minutes I started to get tingling in my fingers and my toes. After a couple more minutes I could actually move my fingers and toes. The feeling was coming back. After what felt like another few minutes, I could pick my arm up. And I moved my legs. This was a big relief. Now I wasn't so scared, the fright sort of ebbed away. Once I could move my arms and legs I thought I was going to be O.K. although I was still complaining about the pain in my head.

The only thing I couldn't move was my head. My head just would not come off the floor. I kept trying. But it wouldn't move.

They must have rung for an ambulance because the Paramedics came and wanted to take my hat off. I remember shouting, "Don't take my hat off!" I had this weird sensation in my head, it felt as if my head would fall off if they took my hat off. I told the Paramedics that I thought I had broken my neck, or my back.

But there was humour even in the midst of all the trauma. Robert Smith asked them which hospital they would be taking me to.

"Liverpool," one of the Paramedics replied.

Whereupon Peter Charles said, "If he's going to Liverpool we'd better take anything valuable off him else he'll come out without it." So he and Robert took my gold Breitling watch off my wrist.

The show ground was a long way down a rough track, when we had come in I had noticed it was quite bumpy with a lot of potholes. The Show Doctor thought that if my neck was broken then I shouldn't have jolts or bumps, I couldn't be taken to hospital in an ordinary ambulance. So they called for an Air Ambulance. This new team of Paramedics arrived and they wanted to take my hat off so they could put a neckbrace on. I still didn't want them to but the Air Ambulance Doctor over-ruled me, he insisted it would be O.K.

When they took my hat off the sensation was amazing. The area of internal bleeding in my head was directly beneath the back edge of my hat. When my hat came off it felt as if my head did fall off, but in fact it was the blood being held back by the pressure of my hat, suddenly falling down my neck.

They gave me gas and air and put me on a stretcher and fitted a neckbrace. Then it was time for my helicopter ride. I knew what to expect, I had been in an Air Ambulance before. The stretcher is pushed in at the back of the helicopter, beneath the rear rotor - the gap where you go through is only about eighteen inches high. If you were claustrophobic you could panic at that stage. But I had learned that the best thing is to just close your eyes and wait until you come out the other side in the cabin.

They flew me to the Countess of Chester Hospital where I was rushed in for X-rays. John and Pat Hales followed, bringing my car to the Hospital. Daniel had phoned Bettina when I was lying on the ground at the show and told her, "Dad has had another fall and he's gone off in the Air Ambulance again, just like at Solihull, but this time I don't think he's very good." Bettina instructed Daniel to go home with the horses and she waited to hear from the hospital. At this stage no one knew what damage had been done.

I went down to X-ray still complaining about the pain, so I was given morphine.

Bettina called my mobile and asked what was the matter with me. I had had too much morphine and had become quite morbid, I was talking gobble de gook. I told her I thought I was going to die. That's how I felt. Bettina said she would drive up to Chester immediately.

I was lying waiting for my X-ray results when John and Pat

arrived. My boots were off but I still had my riding jacket on. The doctor came in and announced, "We can't find anything wrong with you," and I told him, "Well try something else. I'm telling you, I can't move my head, it won't come off the pillow."

So they decided to scan my neck and sure enough it revealed a broken C1, the top vertebrae, broken in two places. That explained why I couldn't move. It was the same type of injury suffered by Christopher Reeve years earlier. They left me there while they decided what to do with me and I remember someone playing with my feet. I could make out a figure at the end of the bed, but I couldn't focus on whom it was. People were talking. Then I saw it was Pat Hales. I remember looking at John but I couldn't think of his name. I don't like morphine, it makes me feel completely out of it, if I can stand the pain I would rather do without.

Mr. Braithwaite, the specialist, came and he told me that I had a pretty serious injury. They would have to put a halo brace on me. I didn't know what the hell a halo brace was but he explained it to me. I didn't like the sound of it.

The nurses cut off my riding jacket and my shirt, they simply chopped them up and got them off. I was taken into a private room and told that they couldn't get a halo for me until Wednesday because each one has to be made to measure. It was now Saturday. They laid me on a board with a thin mattress over it, and strapped my head to the board. Blocks were placed each side of my head and my neck was braced. I spent the next four days strapped to this board.

Bettina arrived and was shocked when she saw me. My good friend Melvyn Barraclough had driven her up and left her so that she could drive my car back. When Daniel had called to tell her I was being taken off in the helicopter, she had phoned Melvyn. He is always there when you need him, and he immediately offered to help. When Pat rang and told her that my neck was broken, Melvyn brought her straight up.

They had me so strapped down that again, I couldn't move. I was fixed on my back. I couldn't move my torso at all, I could only move my arms up and down. At first I said I didn't want to eat but then I had some ice cream which Bettina spoon fed me. After that I felt sick and I was frightened again. If I vomited whilst lying on my back it would be dangerous.

I couldn't watch television, I couldn't sit up. I just lay there for four days. I could hear the television but I couldn't see it. I remember counting the tiles on the ceiling. Every day I counted the tiles, trying to figure out different ways to lay them out. I was so bored.

Every couple of hours the nurses came to roll me. Two of them held my shoulders and head down and another would gently roll the rest of me onto my side, just to move me and release the pressure for a few seconds.

A few people came to see me - my parents both came along with my Aunty Delma; a couple of the lads came in, Peter Murphy, David Bowen, some others, I can't remember clearly; my ex-wife Sarah brought Harry, my youngest son, to see me; Mike Florence brought me a fan - it was September and it was hot. Every day either Pat or John Hales visited, they were both very good. John told me he had bought the horse we had seen on our second shopping trip to Holland. "I've bought Leidi for you. She'll be waiting for you when you get better," he said.

The Parkgate Show paid for a hotel room for Bettina, they were very helpful. She came back next morning and stayed for a couple of days and then on the Wednesday morning my Dad was with me when Mr. Braithwaite and his team came in to fix the halo on my head.

There were six of them and somehow they managed to sit me up; two or three held my head upright and they dressed me in a sheepskin waistcoat with a solid lining; it was fitted around the waist and the top of the shoulders. The sheepskin was to stop me getting sore.

Then they produced this hoop made of titanium and told me what they were going to do next. They were going to screw it into my skull. They placed the hoop on my head, all the while holding me firmly, and gave me a shot of local anaesthetic to freeze the skin where the screws went in.

And then Mr. Braithwaite just screwed the bolts in place. The bolts were like an alan key with a sharp needle point on it. He just kept turning the bolt. I could feel the blood running down my face. He screwed two in my forehead and two in the back of my skull, right into the bone. As a form of torture, I think it would work. Then they inserted four rods, two down the front and two down the back, which went from my chest right up through the halo and out the top. The rods were tightened up until the whole thing was solid and they were happy with it. All the while they were telling me I would make a complete recovery.

Then they let me sit up in bed. The bed was electric and it propped me up. The halo was quite painful and to start with I felt a bit claustrophobic. There was another patient in the Hospital who had a halo fitted and he was meant to come and reassure me that I would soon get used to it but I don't remember seeing him. I felt top heavy, as if I would fall over if I stood up. It was a funny sensation, sitting up after lying down for four days.

When Bettina next came to visit I was sitting in a chair, it was a relief to be out of bed, but when she came in I was asleep, sitting bolt upright with the halo on. She was a bit shocked, it was the first time she had seen it.

Now more visitors started to turn up: Alison Booth, the secretary from Parkgate Show came in every day bringing me whatever I needed, papers, food, I was very grateful to her. All the staff at the hospital were exceptional. I had a good laugh with them and gave the nurses the run around. Breakfast in the morning wasn't very good so one of the nurses used to go off for her own breakfast and bring me sausage sandwiches from the staff canteen.

The next step was walking. A couple of nurses held me up and got me walking around the corridors. They took me for a few trips in a wheel chair at first to get me used to the extra weight on my head. My balance soon improved.

The Olympics were about to start so I watched the Opening Ceremony with Pat Hales and Bettina. I saw John and Michael Whitaker walk past on the television and I rang John. He had his mobile with him and I spoke to them both while the ceremony was on.

And then it was time to go home. Aiden Murphy and Shaun O'Brien, another good mate of mine who owns half shares in a few horses with me, brought Bettina to collect me.

The nurses came to see me off and helped to get me into the car, which was quite difficult because the rods protruded a good few inches above my head. My escort party decided we would not go home down the motorway, we would go along the A roads because it was quieter. This was the worst thing we could have done, at least the motorway would have been a smooth surface. The A roads were so unlevel, every time I went over a bump I had pain in my neck and in my head where the bolts were screwed into my skull.

Back at home my secretary had arranged for me to borrow her mother's electric bed so that I could be propped up in a sitting position. By all accounts it was desperately heavy. Martin Charles, Dobbin, Steve Green and John Botlo all struggled to get the bed into a horsebox and into the drawing room at Finwood Lawn. That is where I slept, for three and a half months.

Robert Smith, my neighbour, was one of my first visitors and I remember telling him that when I was lying on my back I had decided that it no longer mattered whether the poles stayed up or fell down. What was important was to get round without injury, clear or not.

Despite being able to sleep on a washing line, I was finding it difficult to sleep sitting up wearing the halo. The Olympic Games were my saviour because they were televised throughout the night. I would stay awake and watch the most obscure Olympic sports; I became quite an expert on obscure sports.

I was referred to the Royal Orthopaedic in Birmingham and made a couple of visits to the specialist, Mr. Alistair Stirling, to make sure that everything was going on O.K. Every time I had a consultation, they told me I would make a full recovery, I would ride again.

I soon became bored of sitting in bed and decided it was time to go down to the yard. One day, when Bettina was out, I managed to climb into the Discovery, it had plenty of head room, and took myself off down the yard. Of course, it was a stupid thing to do. I only had half a mile to go but if any one had seen me driving through the village they would think there was a monster on the loose. I got a lot of bollockings from everybody for driving.

Especially Bettina. Then I started to go out; I couldn't wear many clothes, just track suit bottoms and a track suit top. The sheep skin itched and I used to shove tea towels up inside to protect my skin. I went to Horse of the Year Show, I didn't look very pretty but people were extremely kind. I used to get tired a lot and although I couldn't sleep at night I would suddenly fall asleep in the day. The halo was great for falling asleep in, your head never wobbled or anything.

And then at about five o'clock one Saturday morning, about ten weeks into the programme, I woke up with an intense pain in my head. It was worse than the pain of the actual fall and I didn't think pain could get any worse than that, but it did. The pain was in the bolt in the left of my forehead. The rod attached to it had somehow come loose and was pushing up against my skull. The only way I could relieve the pain was to pull the rod down, releasing the pressure on my skull.

I told Bettina she'd got to help me so she rang the hospital and Melvyn Barraclough offered to drive us to Birmingham. We had only got to the end of the drive when I couldn't stand it and I climbed out of the car in agony, tears running down my face. Somehow Melvyn got me to the hospital only to find that Mr. Stirling was away and the specialist on duty didn't want to touch the halo. Eventually he took an X-ray to see what was going on and decided to take the halo off and put a hard neck collar on. It was a weird feeling, but once the halo brace was off my neck felt very weak and vulnerable. I knew it had come off too early so I was very careful. I still slept downstairs on the electric bed but I could lie flat which was a relief.

I went for another scan between Christmas and New Year and then went on holiday to Goa with Bettina, the children, Shaun O'Brien and Keeley Durham. I wouldn't get the results of the scan until I returned.

In Goa I was swimming every day and my neck started to feel strong. I took the brace off to swim and it was moving quite well, it felt good. After two weeks of holiday I was really looking forward to going home and riding again, getting the horses ready for the Sunshine Tour.

But when I arrived home there was a message from Mr. Stirling: "Whatever you do, don't ride a horse until you've been to see me."

I was puzzled and wondered what the problem was. I went to see him as soon as possible and he dropped the bombshell. In his opinion, I shouldn't jump again. The vertebrae had healed but the ligament between the bone and the spinal cord had snapped and fallen away, allowing movement. There was no support there. If I fell off a horse again, or had a whip lash injury, the bone could touch the spinal cord and it might be fatal.

I was speechless. The doctors had always told me I would make a full recovery. They suggested I had the top two vertebrae fused to help stabilize it but that would mean my neck would lose 50% of my turning movement, making it impossible to jump anyway.

I came home and told Bettina. I called Lord Harris to tell him the bad news because he had thought I would make a come back with Hopes are High. Lord Harris offered to send me to see another specialist in London. I went to the Blackheath Hospital to see Richard Gullen. He came up with the same prognosis. I was finished.

Bettina came with me to Blackheath and on the drive home we decided I should call it a day. I had no choice. I suppose it was one fall too many.

Nick Skelton's International Show-jumping Achievements

In a career spanning twenty-seven years, Nick Skelton won 1,252 classes, 62 International Grand Prix, appeared on 122 Nations Cup Teams, represented Great Britain in eighteen championships, and won over £4,000,000 in prize money.

JUNIOR EUROPEAN CHAMPIONSHIPS

YEAR	EVENT/VENUE	POSITION/CLASS	HORSE
1974	Lucerne	Team Silver	Maybe
1975	Dornbirn	Team Silver	O.K.
		Individual Gold	O.K.

EUROPEAN CHAMPIONSHIPS

YEAR	EVENT/VENUE	POSITION/CLASS	HORSE
1985	Dinard	Team Gold	St James
1987	St Gallen	Team Gold	Apollo
		Individual Bronze	Apollo
1989	Rotterdam	Team Gold	Apollo/Serenade
1991	La Baule	Team Silver	Phoenix Park
1993	Gijón	Team Silver	Dollar Girl
1995	St Gallen	Team Silver	Dollar Girl
1999	Hickstead		Hopes are High

World Championships

Year	Event/Venue	Position/Class	Horse
1982	Dublin	Team Bronze	If Ever
1986	Aachen	Team Silver	Apollo
1986	Aachen	Individual Bronze	Apollo
1990	Stockholm	Team Bronze	Grand Slam
1994	The Hague	Team Sixth	Dollar Girl
1998	Rome	Team Bronze	Hopes are High

World Cup Final

Year	Event/Venue	Position/Class	Horse
1995	Gothenburg	First	Dollar Girl

Olympic Games

Year	Event/Venue	Position/Class	Horse
1980	Rotterdam	Team Silver (Alt. Olympics)	Maybe
1988	Seoul		Apollo
1992	Barcelona		Dollar Girl
1996	Atlanta		Showtime

Career History

Year	Event/Venue	Position/Class	Horse
1978	HOYS	Leading Show Jumper of the Year	Maybe

Nations Cup Team

Year	Event/Venue	Postion/Class	Horse
	Laxenburg		Lastic
1979	Geneva	1st World Cup Qlfr	Lastic

NATIONS CUP TEAM

YEAR	EVENT/VENUE	POSITION/CLASS	HORSE
	Dublin		Maybe
	Zuidlaren	Team 1st	Maybe
1981	Dublin	2nd World Cup Qlfr	Carat

NATIONS CUP TEAM

YEAR	EVENT/VENUE	POSITION/CLASS	HORSE
	Aachen	Team 1st	Maybe
	Dublin		St James
	Calgary		St James

FEI Bronze Medal Awarded

NATIONS CUP TEAM

YEAR	EVENT/VENUE	POSITION/CLASS	HORSE
1982	Lucerne	Team 1st	If Ever
	Paris		If Ever
	Hickstead		If Ever
1983	Toronto	1st World Cup Qlfr	St James
	Olympia	1st World Cup Qlfr	St James

NATIONS CUP TEAM

YEAR	EVENT/VENUE	POSITION/CLASS	HORSE
	Hickstead		St James
	Paris	Team 1st	St James
	Aachen		If Ever
1984	Royal International	1st King George V	St James

NATIONS CUP TEAM

YEAR	EVENT/VENUE	POSITION/CLASS	HORSE
	Paris	Team 1st	St James
	Dublin		St James
	Rotterdam		Apollo
	Liege	Team 1st	Apollo
	Washington		Apollo
	New York		Apollo
	Toronto		Arabesque

FEI Silver Medal Awarded

YEAR	EVENT/VENUE	POSITION/CLASS	HORSE
1985	Antwerp	1st World Cup Qlfr	St James
	New York	1st World Cup Qlfr	Apollo
	Toronto	1st World Cup Qlfr	Apollo

NATIONS CUP TEAM

YEAR	EVENT/VENUE	POSITION/CLASS	HORSE
	Hickstead	Team 1st	Apollo
	Dublin	Team 1st	Apollo
	Rotterdam		Domino
	Calgary	Team 1st	Apollo
1986	Dortmund	2nd World Cup Qlfr	St James
	Paris	2nd World Cup Qlfr	St James

NATIONS CUP TEAM

YEAR	EVENT/VENUE	POSITION/CLASS	HORSE
	Jerez	Team 1st	Apollo
	Fontainebleau		St James
	Dublin	Team 1st	Apollo
	Rotterdam	Team 1st	Airbourne
	Calgary		Apollo
	Washington	Team 1st	Apollo
	New York		Apollo
	Toronto	Team 1st	Apollo
1987	Hickstead	1st Derby	J Nick

NATIONS CUP TEAM

YEAR	EVENT/VENUE	POSITION/CLASS	HORSE
	Falsterbo		Apollo
	Gijón	Team 1st	Airbourne
	Dublin		Apollo
	Calgary		Apollo
	New York		Apollo
	Toronto		Apollo

FEI Gold Medal Awarded

1988	Hickstead	1st Derby	Apollo
	Dublin	1st Grand Prix	Apollo

NATIONS CUP TEAM

YEAR	EVENT/VENUE	POSITION/CLASS	HORSE
	Rome	Team 1st	Apollo
	Lucerne		Apollo
	Aachen		Apollo
	Dublin	Team 1st	Apollo
	Dinard		Grand Slam
	Rotterdam		Grand Slam
	Calgary		Serenade

1989	Hickstead	1st Derby	Apollo

NATIONS CUP TEAM

YEAR	EVENT/VENUE	POSITION/CLASS	HORSE
	Rome		Apollo
	Hickstead		Apollo
	Geesteren		Apollo
	Luxembourg	Team 1st	Serenade
	Dublin	Team 1st	Grand Slam
	St Gallen	Team 1st	Apollo
	Calgary	Team 1st	Grand Slam
	Seoul		Apollo

1990	Kossen	1st Grand Prix	Fiorella
	Cortina	1st Grand Prix	Fiorella
	Hickstead	2nd Derby	Apollo
	Dublin	1st Grand Prix	Phoenix Park

YEAR	EVENT/VENUE	POSITION/CLASS	HORSE
	Dortmund	1st Grand Prix	Top Gun
	HOYS	1st Grand Prix	Grand Slam

NATIONS CUP TEAM

YEAR	EVENT/VENUE	POSITION/CLASS	HORSE
	Rome	Team 1st	Grand Slam
	Lucerne		Grand Slam
	Aachen		Grand Slam
	Luxembourg		Grand Slam
	Dublin	Team 1st	Phoenix Park
	Rotterdam		Grand Slam
	Calgary	Team 1st	Grand Slam
	New York	Team 1st	Grand Slam
	Toronto		Grand Slam
1991	Hickstead	2nd Derby	Apollo
	HOYS	Leading Show Jumper of the Year	Phoenix Park
	HOYS	Masters	Phoenix Park

NATIONS CUP TEAM

YEAR	EVENT/VENUE	POSITION/CLASS	HORSE
	Rome	Team 1st	Apollo
	Aachen		Apollo
	Luxembourg	Team 1st	Phoenix Park
	Dublin	Team 1st	Phoenix Park
	Calgary	Team 1st	Phoenix Park
	Lanaken		Grand Slam
1992	Dublin	1st Grand Prix	Werra
	Dublin	1st Puissance	Limited Edition
	Gothenburg	1st Grand Prix	Major Wager
	Genk	1st Grand Prix	Major Wager
	Royan	1st Puissance	Limited Edition
	Amsterdam	1st Masters	Limited Edition
	Olympia	Leading Rider	

Nations Cup Team

Year	Event/Venue	Position/Class	Horse
	Lucerne		Limited Edition
	Kappellen		Dollar Girl
	Aachen		Dollar Girl
	Dublin		Limited Edition
	Rotterdam		Limited Edition
	Hickstead	Team 1st	Limited Edition
	Calgary	Team 1st	Dollar Girl
	San Marino		Limited Edition
1993	Royal International	1st King George V	Limited Edition
	Paris	1st World Cup Qlfr	Major Wager
	Paris	1st Grand Prix	Major Wager
	Gothenburg	1st Grand Prix	Major Wager
	Royal Windsor	1st A.I.T	Limited Edition
	Shrewsbury	1st Everest Qlfr	Showtime
	St Gallen	1st Grand Prix	Dollar Girl
	HOYS	1st Everest Final	Showtime
	Ascona	1st Grand Prix	Dollar Girl
	Calgary	1st Du Maurier	Dollar Girl
	Toronto	Leading Rider	Limited Edition

Nations Cup Team

Year	Event/Venue	Position/Class	Horse
	Rome		Dollar Girl
	Hickstead	Team 1st	Limited Edition
	St Gallen		Dollar Girl
	La Baulle		Dollar Girl
	Rotterdam		Limited Edition
	Calgary		Dollar Girl
	San Marino		Limited Edition
	Linz		Showtime
	New York		Limited Edition
	Toronto		Limited Edition
1994	Glasgow	1st Puissance	Limited Edition
	Glasgow	1st Lochinvar Stakes	Dollar Girl
	Millstreet	1st World Cup Qlfr	Dollar Girl

NATIONS CUP TEAM

YEAR	EVENT/VENUE	POSITION/CLASS	HORSE
	Rome		Dollar Girl
	Lucerne		Dollar Girl
	Hickstead		Limited Edition
	Barcelona		Limited Edition
	Dublin	Team 1st	Limited Edition
	Calgary		Dollar Girl
	San Marino		Showtime
1995	Barcelona	1st Grand Prix	Showtime
	Calgary	1st A3	Dollar Girl
	Modena	1st Grand Prix	Showtime
	HOYS	1st Grand Prix	Showtime
	Aarhus	1st A3	Dollar Girl
	Aarhus	1st Masters	Dollar Girl
	Stuttgart	1st Grand Prix	Dollar Girl
	Stuttgart	1st Hit & Hurry	Sublime
	Olympia	Leading Rider	
	Olympia	2nd World Cup Qlfr	Dollar Girl

NATIONS CUP TEAM

YEAR	EVENT/VENUE	POSITION/CLASS	HORSE
	Rome		Dollar Girl
	Aachen		Dollar Girl
	Luxembourg		Showtime
	Dublin		Showtime
	Rotterdam		Showtime
	Calgary		Dollar Girl
	San Marino		Sublime
1996	Bordeaux	1st World Cup Qlfr	Dollar Girl
	Bordeaux	1st 2 Fence Challenge	Cathleen III
	Royal International	1st King GeorgeV	Cathleen III
	Geneva	3rd World Cup Final	Dollar Girl
	Dublin	1st A3	Dollar Girl
	Moorsele	1st Grand Prix	Dollar Girl
	Madrid	1st Grand Prix	Showtime
	Gijón	1st Power & Speed	Sublime
	Munich	1st = Topscore	Sublime
	Gijón	1st Grand Prix	Dollar Girl
	Gijón	1st Hunting	Sublime

Year	Event/Venue	Position/Class	Horse
	Bremmen	1st Hunting	Dollar Girl
	Stuttgart	1st Hit & Hurry	Sublime
	Geesteren	1st A4	Quick Star
	Geesteren	1st Hunting	Quick Star
	Olympia	1st Masters	Zalza
	Olympia	1st Xmas Stocking	Quick Star

Nations Cup Team

Year	Event/Venue	Position/Class	Horse
	Lisbon	Team 1st	Cathleen III
	Luxembourg		Sublime
	Dublin	Team 1st	Dollar Girl
	Gijón		Dollar Girl
	Calgary	Team 1st	Showtime
1997	Monte Carlo	Leading Rider	(Various horses)
	Monte Carlo	1st A3	Showtime
	Royal Windsor	1st Hildon	Tinka's Boy
	Madrid	1st Hunting	Zalza
	Madrid	1st A4	Showtime
	Lisbon	1st Grand Prix	Showtime
	Rotterdam	1st A3	Showtime
	Leeuwarden	1st Accumulator	Cartagene
	HOYS	1st Grand Prix	Showtime
	HOYS	1st Traxdata Challenge	Showtime
	HOYS	1st 6 & 7-year-old	Cartagene
	Olympia	1st Xmas Stakes	Showtime
	Olympia	1st Take Your Own Line	J.J.
	Bordeaux	2nd World Cup Qlfr	Zalza

Nations Cup Team

Year	Event/Venue	Position/Class	Horse
	La Baule		Tinka's Boy
	Royal Windsor	Team 1st	Showtime
	Lisbon		Showtime
	Modena	Team 1st	Showtime
	Gijón	Team 1st	Tinka's Boy
	Dublin		Showtime

YEAR	EVENT/VENUE	POSITION/CLASS	HORSE
1998	Grenoble	1st A4	Cartagene
	Aldershot	1st International Trial	Showtime
	Madrid	1st Grand Prix	Showtime
	Madrid	1st Power & Speed	Showtime
	Madrid	1st A2	Cartagene
	Moorsele	2nd Power & Speed	Cartagen
	Royal Windsor	1st Open	Cartagene
	Gijón	1st Grand Prix	Hopes are High
	Royal International	2nd King George V	Hopes are High
	Dublin	1st Grand Prix	Hopes are High
	Spruce Meadows	1st Du Maurier	Hopes are High
	Spruce Meadows	2nd A3	Showtime
	Leeuwarden	1st Grand Prix	Zalza
	Millstreet	1st A4	Showtime
	Gijón	1st Grand Prix	Hopes are High
	Gijón	1st Power & Speed	Showtime
	Gijón	1st A4	Showtime
	Gijón	2nd Hunting	Cartagene
	Stuttgart	2nd A4	Zalza
	Olympia	1st Xmas Hamper	Showtime

NATIONS CUP TEAM

YEAR	EVENT/VENUE	POSITION/CLASS	HORSE
	La Baule		Giselle
	Lisbon		Giselle
	Dublin		Hopes are High
	Gijón		Hopes are High
	Spruce Meadows		Hopes are High
1999	Royal International	1st King George V	Hopes are High
	Royal International	2nd July Stakes	Showtime
	Dublin	3rd Grand Prix	Hopes are High

NATIONS CUP TEAM

YEAR	EVENT/VENUE	POSITION/CLASS	HORSE
	Modena		Hopes are High
	Hickstead	Team 2nd	Hopes are High
	Dublin	Team 2nd	Hopes are High

YEAR	EVENT/VENUE	POSITION/CLASS	HORSE
	Calgary		Hopes are High
2000	Royal Windsor	1st Gentlemen's Champ	Jalisco
	Royal Windsor	1st Grand Prix	Jalisco
	Barcelona	1st A4	Jalisco
	Barcelona	1st Accumulator	Showtime
	Madrid	1st A4	Jalisco
	Madrid	1st Accumulator	Showtime
	Berkshire	2nd International Trial	Lalique
	Hickstead	2nd Derby Tankard	Showtime
	Hickstead	2nd Zangersheide	Lalique

NATIONS CUP TEAM

YEAR	EVENT/VENUE	POSITION/CLASS	HORSE
	Lisbon		Lalique

MAJOR GRAND PRIX WINS

VENUE	NUMBER OF WINS
Aachen	3
Antwerp	1
Ascona	1
Barcelona	2
Calgary	3
Cortina	1
Dortmund	1
Dublin	5
Geneva	1
Genk	1
Gijón	2
Gothenburg	2
Hickstead	5
Hickstead Derby	3
Jerez	2
Kossen	2
Leeuwarden	2
Lisbon	1
Madrid	2
Millstreet	2
Modena	1
Moorsele	1

VENUE	NUMBER OF WINS
New York	2
Olympia	3
Paris	1
's Hertogenbosch	1
St Gallen	1
Stuttgart	1
Toronto	2
HOYS	2
Windsor	4
Zuidlaren	1

Warming up at a Show

At shows, I always worked the horses early in the morning, at seven or eight o'clock, before classes started. I never believed in getting on a horse and working it for fifteen minutes or so before it jumped. I believe the flat work should be done in the morning.

I would get on my horse at the point in the class when there were twelve to go before me. If I was first to go I would get on twenty minutes before the class was due to start. I would do flat work for five minutes, trotting and cantering. Then I would walk around the collecting ring, making sure I could remember the course.

I would start jumping practice when there were seven horses to go. At that point I would get off and pull the saddle forward. I was finnicky, I could never get far enough forward, I hate it when the saddle goes back, I always liked to sit on their ears.

When there were two horses to go before me I would jump one small oxer.

With one horse to go I would jump one big vertical. And then I would go into the ring.

That is what I did with every horse. That's how I warmed them up, all the years I competed. I had a system and I stuck to that system, day in day out. I never changed.

Working horses at home

I would usually be down at the yard ready to start riding at eight o'clock in the morning, sometimes earlier. I like the horses to be worked or hacked in the morning and back in their stables by lunchtime.

When I worked a horse, I worked it. I didn't just ride around the place, I made sure the horse worked. I could do more work on a horse in ten minutes than some people do in an hour.

I always rode with draw reins. Not everybody agrees with that method but it worked for me. I could work well with draw reins and I knew how to use them. They can be dangerous, people say they aren't good as they are an artificial aid but to my way of thinking, 'If you can do it in half an hour in draw reins, why take an hour without them.' The less stress a horse puts on his joints over the years, the better. But draw reins in the wrong hands are like giving a monkey a razor blade.

In the ring, I always tried to ride my horses in a mild bit but I would train and work them at home in a more severe bit.

Stable Management

My horses are looked after like they are living in a hotel. They have the best food. I used to be quite old fashioned about feeding: I liked bran, oats, nuts, chaff. It was only very recently that I decided the feed manufacturers had got it right and changed my horses on to mix.

I like to know how much my horses are drinking and how often they drink. I won't have automatic water bowls.

I insist that hooves are meticulously picked out and greased every day.

Ever since farmers started making haylage I have always fed it. There is no dust or waste and because it comes ready-wrapped it is easily transported to a show.

The horses are bedded down on shavings and the floors of the stables are made of dirt. Dirt floors drain well, so it is more economical on shavings and horses don't knock their hocks on the concrete floors. No need for rubber floors!

Tack

My horses have the best tack and rugs. I don't like rugs with neck covers, I find they take the mane off.

I like to see all the keepers in place and I hate bridles that don't fit: the noseband is hanging off, or it's not adjusted level as you look at it. I remember David Bowen telling his groom off one time. The noseband was very loose, it was doing no good at all and he said, ' 'Ere lass, do that nose band up tight. What would happen if you didn't do your bra up tight? Your tits would fall out, wouldn't they love?'

I always rode with continental reins, made of webbing with leather stops. You can keep your grip, the reins don't slip.

I prefer leather girths, but not elasticated ones. With an elasticated girth you can just keep pulling and pulling and when do you stop? Eventually your horse can't breathe.

The saddle pad should be big enough to reach a good two inches clear of the cantle of the saddle, and pulled up into the pommel space a couple of inches. I don't like to see a saddle pad right underneath the cantle of the saddle, otherwise when you sit on it the edge rubs into the horses back.

I like horses to wear front boots to protect their tendons and if they knock themselves then put back boots on, but not otherwise.

Rider's equipment

I hardly ever carried a whip, maybe I would on a stallion but I rarely took a whip into the ring. I can't see the need for them. Give the horse a good kick instead. Ride more strongly with your legs. Horses stop for a reason, there's no point hitting it in the ring if it stops. I don't like to see horses, or ponies for that matter, being pulled about in the mouth and knocked around in the ring. I don't think it does the horse any good and it's definitely not good for the image of the sport.

I didn't like anybody using my spurs, I was funny about them. I used to bend them myself so they were exactly how I wanted them and they felt comfortable. To this day they are still hanging in the tack room, and nobody, but nobody, is allowed to use them.

I don't know what I'm saving them for, but there you are.